FACES OF AGING

Nader Robert Shabahangi, Ph.D.

FACES OF AGING

©2002 *Elders Academy Press*

All rights reserved. No part of this publication may be reproduced or transmitted in any form or by any means, electronic or mechanical, including photography, recording, or any information storage and retrieval systems without written permission in writing from the publisher, except by a reviewer written for inclusion in a magazine, newspaper, or broadcast.

Published by Elders Academy Press
Published and printed in Warsaw, Poland

Elders Academy Press
ul. Baluckiego 12
02-604 Warszawa
Poland

www.pacificinstitute-europe.org
www.pacificinstitute.org

ISBN 83-917996-0-3

*If I could tell you what it meant,
there would be no point in dancing it.*

~ Isadora Duncan

THIS WORK IS DEDICATED

TO THE CAREGIVERS

AND SUPPORT STAFF OF

HAYES VALLEY CARE

To Cristina Abebe, Adnan Sharif, Elsy Barrera, Janet Cabuntala, Sonia Calderon, Juan Cante, Perla Cerpa, Henry Chua, Yanira Cortez, Wilma De la Cruz, Szilvia Druskoczi, Nelo Dychangco, Edith Finch, Roger Grafil, Guadalupe Guillen, JeannaLyn Gutierrez, Tagreed Haddad, Marly Honorato, Eugene Malari, Letecia Manulat, Francisco Marques, Alma Martinez, Lionel Melchor, Sandra Melchor, Elmer Mikery, John Mohler, Harriet Noguerra, Dolores Nucal, Erlinda Padua, Milagros Paredes, Linda De Trinidad Perez, Katia Petkova, Carlos Pinello, Sannie Prado, Maira Ramirez, Blanca Reyes, Norma Robertson, Gonzalo Santiago, Ovet Sera Josef, Katherine Sulit, Francisco Tejada, Victoria Tuvilla, Gloria Verano, Leslie Wright, Luz Zalameda – and to all those who have helped us in the past and are not named here.

TABLE OF CONTENTS

About the Photography — viii

A Word about and by the Poets — ix

Foreword — xi

Introduction

Discovering the World of the Elderly:
Building Hayes Valley Care — 1

Questioning the Faces of Aging — 8

Part I

Seeing Differently — 14

Part II

The Inner Elder — 36

Part III

On Becoming an Elder — 48

Notes — 68

Acknowledgements — 71

ABOUT THE PHOTOGRAPHY

The images you see in these pages are those of residents of Hayes Valley Care, a residence and community for seniors. Over the years I have taken pictures of the residents because I have always loved taking pictures, especially portraits. The more I looked at the faces of aging, the more beautiful they became. It began to dawn on me that the faces I was seeing were faces that spanned the 20th century, faces that were part of an uncanny century of changes and experiences. At times I was envious of what they had experienced, what they already knew. At other times I admired their calm and their way of being.

I am shy at taking pictures. This is why the photos in this book are taken informally during special occasions and festivities held at Hayes Valley Care.

~Nader

A WORD ABOUT AND BY THE POETS

The poems in this book were written by Cliff and Julia Landis. Cliff is a Residential Life Coordinator and Julia an activities therapist and spirituality consultant at Hayes Valley Care. Cliff came to us first as an intern who wanted to work with the elderly and soon became so involved and passionate that he made it his full-time occupation. His ability to allow the elderly to be themselves, his sensitivity to their world and needs is remarkable. Julia began as a trainer for our caregivers at Hayes Valley Care and soon became as dedicated to working with the elderly as her partner Cliff. She continually places her gift and skills as a therapist and healer in their service. Julia and Cliff's exceptional humanity and sensitivity shine through in their poetic work.

Introduction to Our Poems

"Writing a poem about a subject gives us an opportunity to reflect deeply. Writing about the residents, people we already felt we knew, gave us the chance to contemplate their life: their beauty, their struggles and inner riches.

Over and over, we found unexpected depth in simple encounters. We were touched by meaning inherent in the simple things of each resident's world – a hat, a gesture, an expression.

Nothing was just itself. Through these things, and in living ordinary moments with them, we began to feel the essential, unique quality of each life. We joined that world with our memory and imagination in our writing process.

This journey brought forth a deeper respect for each of these people. It reminded us of the eternal quality of each life, *a suchness* beyond impermanence and mortality.

We hope that in reading these poems you might feel that you have known the people pictured here and be touched by them."

~ Julia & Cliff

FOREWORD

Old age tends to be associated with decay and weakness. We can learn to change this attitude towards aging. This takes preparation, however.

Rather than being "just" old, we can learn to become elders who offer maturity and depth. Rather than feeling useless, we can become a vital and thus all-important part of our culture and society.

What if we couldn't wait to be old, just like a child can't wait to be an adult?

This book is for anyone who is intrigued by such a prospect.

INTRODUCTION

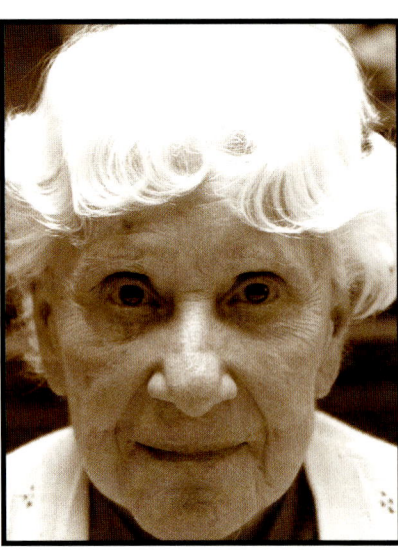

FACES OF AGING

DISCOVERING THE WORLD OF THE ELDERLY: BUILDING HAYES VALLEY CARE

Having grown up in a rural environment in northern Germany where (at least at the time) the elderly were afforded a healthy dose of respect, I was stunned to see how the elderly in the United States were treated and viewed. I could not imagine struggling through a lifetime of travail only to end up in that cold and callous environment that was now being reserved for such a large section of the elderly population. I saw the elderly being gathered in warehouse-style nursing homes, where many of them sat unnoticed for hours under the anaesthetizing flickering of fluorescent hallway lights, and where – more importantly – they were seen and treated as useless members of society. This was a rude awakening, something I had not expected to find in such a "civilized" country as the United States. I began to do my part to change the situation.

The overriding purpose of this book is to look at the aging process with a fresh eye and an open heart. There is a personal and a social-activist bent to the following pages. The personal aspect has to do with my being close to the elderly on a daily basis. It is a closeness that often gets me thinking about how I would like to be and live during my so-called golden years. Meanwhile, the social activist in me takes a dim view of how the elderly are generally viewed and treated in this society.

But there is also a third dynamic at play. Maybe we can call this a spiritual dimension. I believe there is more to life than the material realm. Beyond the simplified worldview provided by the modern scientific attitude – an attitude that represses realities other than those it knows how to manipulate – lie other dimensions important to human life. These dimensions manifest for those who allow themselves to be close to the elderly.

I was finishing my doctorate when I first experienced the world of the elderly in the United States. I actually began working with the elderly by happenstance. My friends needed help expanding their board-and-care home. Their home was exemplary, a beautiful old building overlooking the Pacific Ocean, with a rose garden on the outside and a warm interior and caring friends and staff inside. But I was soon shocked when I began visiting other care homes in search of ideas to expand my friends' place. The housing and treatment conditions were dismal, and I understood that the familiar phrase of the "warehousing of the elderly" was no exaggeration. Already during the expansion of my friends' place, I assigned myself the mission of building a home that fulfilled the vision of truly respectful care for the elderly.

The result was Hayes Valley Care, named after a neighborhood in San Francisco that borders on the Civic Center area. My two brothers and I launched the design and construction of this project with little more than sheer determination and a few dollars from our savings and credit cards. As it turned out, the stars were aligned in our favor. We opened the doors only two years later, and within another year we had turned the place into a home that answered our dreams and became a successful business.

After Hayes Valley Care's first year of operations, we launched construction of a restaurant on the home's premises. The idea was to serve the home's residents with quality food in a restaurant setting that could also double as a place where residents and their friends and families could come together. It was important that the care home not be a segregated entity such as an "adult-only community" in some suburb. We wanted the elderly to be integrated as vital members of the community. The restaurant would bring the "outer community" (the public) into the care home, while the "inner community" (the elderly residents, support staff and residents' families) would be able to freely integrate with the outer community.

The idea of the restaurant gave rise to *Terra Brazilis*, a Brazilian restaurant with innovative food and a warm, inviting atmosphere – just the place to meet and relax with friends and family.

Restaurant aside, the central vision behind Hayes Valley Care was to provide sound emotional care to its elderly residents. This, in fact, was a main element that we found wanting among many of the other care providers we visited. Hayes Valley Care teamed up with the Pacific Institute, a non-profit counseling and research center, and began a psychology internship program that trained and supervised psychotherapy students who would be working with the elderly.

We started with one student and increased the number progressively. We ensured that our elderly residents gained increasing contact with these eager and social members of the younger generation. As part of this "gerontological wellness program" (as it was called in the early days), we placed strong emphasis on breaking out of the traditional therapeutic approach, which was to engage and "cure" clients by applying specific methods and techniques. We believed that by applying more existential-humanistic and process-oriented principles, we could stay closer to the residents' emotional core. In our relations with the elderly, we championed a being-with rather than a doing-to type of interaction.

The next component close to our hearts was a desire to make space for the spirit at Hayes Valley Care. Through a friend, some of our Hayes Valley Care staff members were invited to the *Blue Mountain Center of Meditation*, a place founded by Eknath Easwaran and that promotes "The Life of the Spirit."

We were introduced to just the non-denominational spiritual program we wanted for Hayes Valley Care. We began to envision how we could implement these ideas at our residence. The program emphasized such states of mind and behavior as inwardness and quieting the mind through daily meditation practice; reading the writings of the great mystics, saints and other wise and reflective thinkers who have endured the test of time; striving for single-mindedness; focusing on the task at hand without allowing oneself to be distracted – such as, for instance, concentrating on eating alone without reading the paper or listening to music or talking to someone else. To incorporate a spiritual dimension to caring for our elderly, we were aware that we needed the support of Hayes Valley Care residents, staff members, caregivers and administration,

as well as of professionals from our local community and from other communities. We also knew that we needed to overcome plenty of societal and cultural preconceptions regarding "spiritual programs."

One such preconception was that there should be no place for religious or spiritual beliefs in the workplace, that people should only be free to display their spiritual or religious leanings in places of worship and at home, but not in public. There was also resistance from within the professional health-care community. Many psychotherapists, social workers, physicians and private and public guardians bristle at the notion of a spiritual program.

On top of this, we had to address some well-justified fears that the right of religious freedom – which by extension involves the right of non-religious freedom – could be impinged upon. As some of our elderly residents were quite fragile, the fear of spiritual ideas being imposed upon them was understandable. Human history is filled with religious oppression and holy crusades and atrocities committed in the name of God. After all, religious persecution and conflict continue to this day.

We are still in the process of implementing a non-denominational program at Hayes Valley Care. It is hard to underestimate the issue's importance. Roughly 80% of Americans believe in the importance of the spirit, and we know that especially during older age, spiritual questions are a major concern for a substantial portion of society.[1] And we know that unless the elderly feel safe to voice their spiritual needs, they simply will not express them. They will fear that there is no one to listen to or to understand them, and they will fear being ridiculed. It is for this reason that we continue to search for ways of making space for the spirit so that our especially more fragile residents, who are unable to leave the home, can freely express their needs for spiritual assertion and practice.

Most of what we do at Hayes Valley Care is anchored by a desire to take up the challenge of allowing for a richness and diversity of being. Allowing this richness means learning to accept the diversity of human life. This desire finds its expression at Hayes Valley Care and is supported by our staff, the people at the Pacific Institute and the interns who come to work with us every year.

Still, it is not easy to translate the goal of "richness of being" into everyday practice of care for the elderly. This is more than a theoretical discussion on the problems of aging or the pros and cons of growing old. The concern transcends the theoretical. I would like to continue to stimulate my community and anyone who reads this book to address the question of how to allow for "the richness of being old."

Saying the Nevers

Still...
We'll never be young again.

That's a hard word: *Never.*
Never say Never.
Wrong.
Need to say it now. Selectively, of course.
I'll never be young again.
I'll never have that perfect body.
I'll never know all there is to know.
I'll never do all I meant to do.
I'll never see all I wanted to see.
I'll never be as noble as I hope to to be.
I'll never be famous.
I'll never be 'first.'
I'll never be a hero.
I'll never see my grandchildren grow old.
Never... never... never... never...

Yes, say them all.

Because *Someday…*
and *Maybe…*
and *Perhaps…*
keep us dangling over into tomorrows
using up our time
taking up precious space.

Pining over yesterday
Longing for another chance at youth
Pretending away the years
Wastes whatever we have left to spend.

Never sweeps clean.
Never leaves room for something else.

I'll never be young again means
we get to be older, even *Old*.
We've never done that before.
It's a new adventure.
No, says the youngster inside us.
Try it out, says the adventurer,
always ready for a different experience.

~Elizabeth Bugental
Agesong[2]

QUESTIONING THE FACES OF AGING

In my work with the elderly I have discovered that my attitudes towards them reflect attitudes I hold towards myself. James Hillman uses the term inner elder, which suggests that each of us possesses an elder within. Our inner elder – when allowed to be a part of our lives – can guide us forward and draw us onward. The way our society views and treats its elderly is an indication of how we treat our inner elders. It should not come as a surprise that so much of our generation feels lost and unguided.

If I ask questions about the prevailing mindset that has allowed the elderly I have seen in homes and on the streets to be treated disrespectfully, I might as well ask myself why I treat my own inner elder so badly.

If I question what makes the elderly so invisible in today's society, I might as well ask why I cannot find a center within myself, or why I have a hard time hearing my own inner voice.

Maybe I am wondering why the elderly are viewed through certain lenses of understanding that do not allow them to be who they are. If that is my concern, I might as well ask myself which unconscious preconceptions guide my life. In other words, I myself live within "boxes" of which I remain unaware.

Humans are influenced greatly by the images they perceive. Advertisements, television and the movie industry all exploit this influence. External images often shape the images we have of ourselves. In terms of concrete images, let us call them "the faces of aging." In our culture, there are scant images of elders that give us an idea of what it is to be an elder. Yet there is a strong need for such images. Kenneth Lakritz points out that the "younger generations bear the responsibility of laboring physically, emotionally and spiritually to cultivate a new world, and they are crucially in need of mature guidance to initiate them into deeper awareness in the midst of the confusion in their lives. We [adults] expect that they somehow, without guidance, become more mature than we ourselves are."[3]

Many of us in our "middle years," for example, feel that something is missing, that we have skills and talents but that somehow those skills and talents are not being put to use in the best possible way. More simply, many of us feel that there is more to life than earning a living. I read of one biologist who quit her job and journeyed to a Greek Island to "find herself;" every night she stretched out her arms to the vast universe around her and exclaimed a simple yet urgent plea: "Use me!"

We know that something is wrong, that something is off, but we can't seem to put our finger on it.

To whom can we turn? We have lost faith in the experts, the professionals and the politicians. Who has not been corrupted? Who has not been bought, or is not out for his or her own interest, or is not merely following the latest trend or fashion? We have taught ourselves to believe that we can trust only ourselves. But do we have the wisdom, the life experience, and the maturity to guide us along life's path? If we did, would we be so worried about questions of what to do or feel next?

The image of the wise elder throughout human history and mythology has served as the voice of the trusted. Schachter-Shalomi writes:

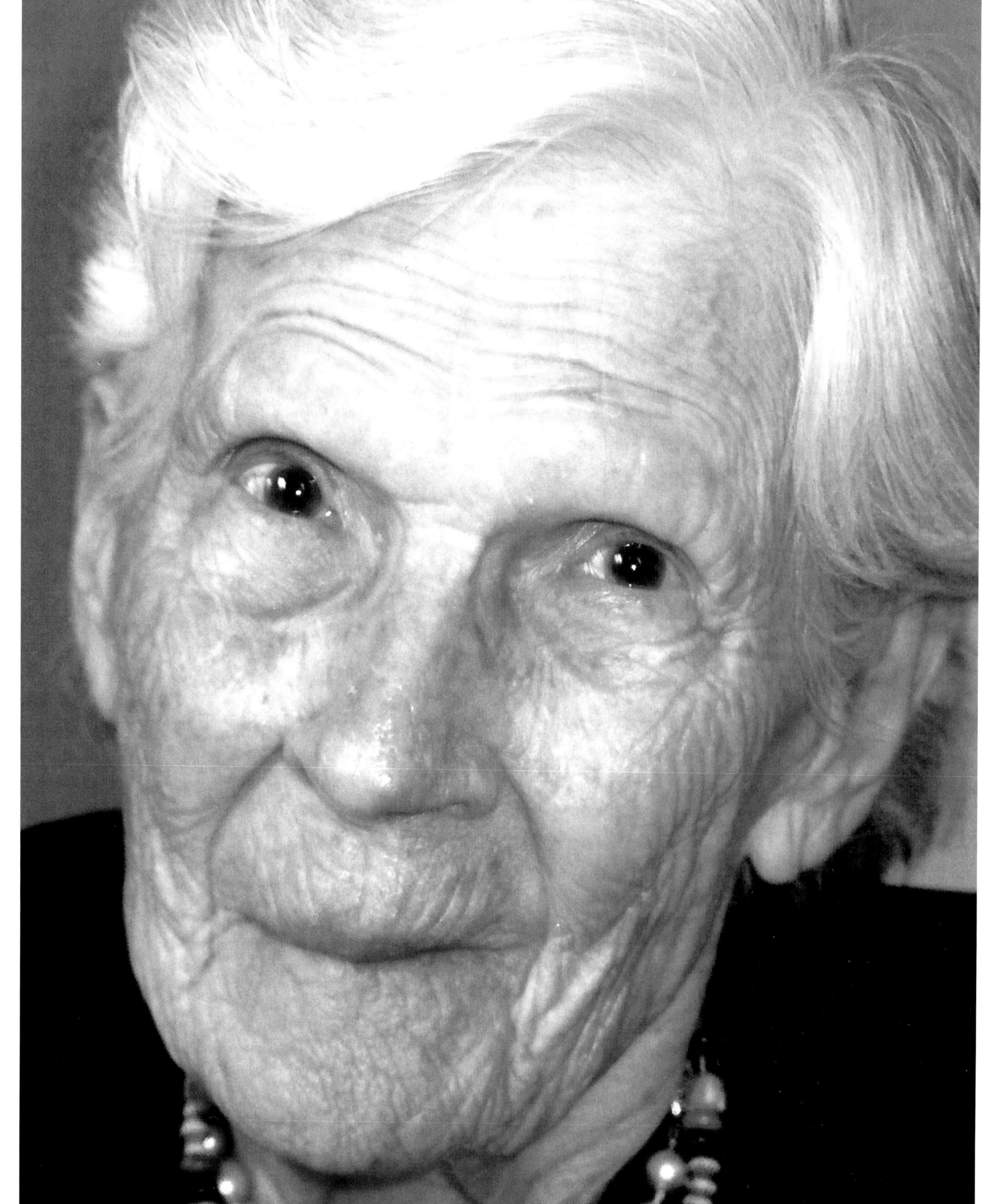

"To become our unique selves rather than second-hand imitations, we need someone standing behind us, saying, as it were, 'I bless you in the heroic, worthwhile, and difficult task of becoming yourself.' Such a person evokes our questing spirit, not by giving answers, but by deepening our ability to question and to search for meaning. As we work through anxiety, doubt, and occasional discouragement in our quest for a genuine life path, our [elder] acts as a midwife, helping us to breathe more easily as we give birth to ourselves in the world."[4]

Fairy-tales abound with images of wise elderly people. An old man or woman often appears at a difficult moment, imparting the very nugget of advice that the hero needs. The elder's wisdom helps the hero out of a seemingly impossible situation and protects the hero from outer dangers or inner weakness.

Of course, there are other old characters: wicked, rigid, waiting to trap a young hero or heroine, striving to stave off anything new or different or creative.

The following two polar extremes describe what Hillman calls a *senex* archetype: "Senex means sixty, and it also means the old, the aged. Now, the senex includes both the older and the elder, which are different aspects of this whole complex. In other words, with the elder you associate the qualities of wisdom, knowledge, and guidance, but you also have the older, which includes the bitter, limiting, judgmental, dismissive qualities of a person... ."[5]

Our culture tends to emphasize the negative characteristics of old age, which makes both the process of aging and the finding of an inner guide difficult. As Ram Dass puts it:

"The images our culture generates are designed to make you feel that aging is a kind of a failure; that somehow God made a big mistake. If only God was as smart as the commercials, people would be young forever... ."[6]

So Many Questions…

Again, the purpose of this book is to look at the aging process with a fresh eye and an open heart. We often ignore the elderly or treat them with carelessness. Where and how did we learn this? What has led so many of the elderly to describe themselves as useless members of society? What are the forces at work within us (what might be called consensus reality) that create such a self-degrading perception as that expressed by the word "useless"? If someone describes himself as useless, then somewhere there must lie an operative definition of "useful." Who or what decides on these definitions? And to what end?

And More Questions…

How can we as a society allow the elderly to grow in a way that they wish to grow? How can we let them be who they are, and let them live the things they want to live in their final years? There is a certain impatience when gerontologist Gunhild O. Hagestad asks:

"When will it be acknowledged that even in advanced old age, millions of people function independently? When will it be recognized that most old people do not represent dependency and a drain on familial and societal resources,

but rather that they indeed constitute a vastly underutilized social resource? When will it be grasped and realized that there are rich new possibilities presented by recent demographic and social changes?"[7]

We need to ask ourselves how, in our care for the elderly, we constrain the very subjects of that care due to our personally and culturally generated ideas of what it means to be old and what is acceptable or appropriate for the elderly. How do we remain conscious of the ways in which we impose our own fears of aging, of death, of the changes that invariably occur as we age, onto the elderly themselves? Here, again, if we ask ourselves to face our own fears of aging and dying, maybe we can begin to understand how these fears express themselves in our work with, and attitudes toward, the elderly. It is not easy work, but every one of us does eventually have to confront these questions.

And yet another question: How, in our interactions with the elderly, can we remain open to what they have to offer us, not only because they have more life experience than we do, but also because they are entrusted in our care? Here the concept of the inner elder might be helpful. What does it mean to be talking about our inner elder? Who is he (or she)? How does our contact with the elderly inform our awareness of our own inner elders? How is the whole topic of the elderly important to those of us in the younger generations? How is this subject important to the way that we live our lives, or to the world around us? Or is it?

These questions come dressed in many forms throughout this book. They are not meant to be conclusively answered, because by their very nature such answers vary from person to person. Therefore, this book raises more questions than answers. The goal is to encourage the reader to ponder the many issues that confront us when we think of the elderly, when we need to care for an elderly person, and/or would like to make contact with our own inner elder.

Part *One* will look at how we treat the elderly in our culture and examine our common assumptions about aging. We will look at the typical images of the elderly, discuss the "boxes" in which we place them, and ask how we might open them up. We will see what we can learn from and with the elderly.

Part *Two* travels inward to study the concept of the "inner elder." Here I will pose some questions that might help us search for this "wise guide" that dwells somewhere within us.

Part *Three* sets forth a task for those of us who would prefer to become elders rather than simply old. This is not only a challenge for the individual, it is also a hope for society: to age with awareness; to integrate that which is eternally fresh and young within us with that special brand of wisdom that we gain from life experience; to remain open to all parts of ourselves; and to be willing to give what we have to offer to others.

This desire to stir up our processes of thinking and feeling about the many faces of aging also turns this project into a book of images of the elderly. You are invited to ponder these images, see what they mean to you. Let the images of the elderly also speak for themselves, free of words or preconceptions.

PART ONE • SEEING DIFFERENTLY

Look at the face of an older person. What do you see? What do you feel? What if you did not have the word "old" to describe that face? What if wrinkles did not mean old, but signaled the depth of life this person has experienced? People often sense a degree of fear when they see an old face. What if they instead felt a sense of longing to have what that older person has? What if power and money were not considered the highest possible awards, but maturity was? And what if maturity was a term only reserved for the very old, those who have lived a truly full life and have proven that they had the strength to age by not just accepting but embracing their aging as perhaps the richest part of their lives? What if we couldn't wait to be old, just like a child cannot wait to be an adult?

Let us break open the boxes in which our culture has placed the elderly. Doing so will serve not only the elderly of today, but also the elderly of tomorrow. Breaking open the boxes, beating down the stereotypes of what we see when we look at the elderly, is a personal endeavor as much as it is social activism. I shudder at the thought that as I grow older society will value me less; or even worse, that I will value myself less; or that when, at 70, I might indulge in a little harmless social monkey business only to earn myself a chorus of disapproving glances. I do not want people to stare at me when, at 80 and while riding the bus, I choose to give my girlfriend a peck on the cheek. I do not want students at, for instance, some university rally, to dismiss what I say because I am deemed to be too old to know the score. If I whistle a song in the supermarket, I would prefer it if the spry 40-year old at the cash register did not take it as ill-mannered behavior. When I walk down the street, I do not want to notice that no one looks at me anymore, and when I drive my car, I can do without loud honking and a livid motorist behind me shouting that I'm an old fart who should stay off the roads. And I don't want to have to be extra-careful at the cash machine, or go to a party only to be seen as a person who is of no interest to anyone present.

If, as a white male in his so-called prime, I feel myself into being an older person in today's society, then I begin to realize that the experiences I fear mirror those of many of this society's minorities and other marginalized groups. These groups have been talking for decades about being ignored, shunned, disapproved of, intimidated, ridiculed and mistreated. The experience of growing old has become for many the experience of becoming just that kind of outcast.

This experience has been in the making for some time now. In the nineteenth century, medicine began to classify old age as a disease, a period of moral and mental decrepitude. Modern industry had (and has) little use for those who it judges to be less willing or able to be exploited by long and intense hours of labor. Capitalism and the free market have little use for those who do not purchase and consume to the degree that they once did. Research links increased modernization to a decrease in the elderly's social status and a fraying of the traditional attitudes toward responsibility and care for them. The demise of the extended family in modern, industrialized countries, with a trend toward moving the grandparents out of the house and (often) into isolation is an example of this shift in attitude.

Not that there was ever a golden age of the elderly.[8] Life expectancy has indeed improved significantly, from for instance 47 years in mid-19th-century Germany, to the high seventies today. It was in fact Otto von Bismarck who invented 65 as the retirement age in his social program because statistically most people were dead by then. Until relatively recently, a rather small portion of society lived to retirement age. Today, thanks to medical science and a host of other factors, great steps have been taken in treating the elderly and in managing chronic pain, resulting in an increase in life expectancy.

Conflicted Past

Note that the respect that the older members of a family received within their family circle often went hand in hand with oppression of the families' younger members by these very elders.[9] This makes the issue of respecting the elderly much more complex and emotionally charged. When a a young person feels mistreated or even abused by an older person, this experience can be difficult to undo. Can this abuse of power – at least partially – be connected to the loss of power the elderly have experienced in the last generations?

The Elderly: As Diverse as Other Groups

It is important to note that when we talk about the elderly we are not talking about a homogeneous group of people. Much has been researched on and written about the heterogeneity of the elderly based on their birthplace, ethnicity, race, gender, social class or financial status.[10] Just as there is an unfathomable diversity in character and personality among the younger generations, the same diversity exists among the elderly.

Becoming Conscious of the Box

Freud's dictum of "where id is, let ego be" (or, in other words, let us become conscious of that which is still unconscious) begs the following question: How can we as individuals, as a culture and society and through our politics, remain aware of this amazing diversity among the elderly? Whether it is a part of basic human nature to quickly identify and label the unknown, or whether it is a fashion of modern societies (or even a combination of the two), we like to stick labels on one another and impose certain norms and expectations. The pain and suffering of many minority groups in the United States can attest to this. As Mike Hepworth states, the "belief that life can be differentiated into a number of phases, each with its own definitive characteristics interconnected by appropriate transitions or status passages," is itself a structure of thinking that is in need of revision.[11]

It is worth looking at some of the structures of thinking that tend to marginalize the elderly.

We Are not Only Our Bodies

Growing older is not a burden, but a part of a continued personal and spiritual unfolding. Society's basic idea of treating the aging process as a nuisance, as something to be avoided, results mainly from the fact that we mistakenly focus on aging as a process of the body's weakening. We identify who we are with our bodies. This point of view is a mindset that can turn growing older into an unnecessarily difficult experience since our society tends to idealize the fit and productive, strong and agile, shiny and wrinkle-free body. There is no escaping the biological

GROWING OLDER IS NOT A BURDEN, BUT PART OF A CONTINUED PERSONAL AND SPIRITUAL UNFOLDING

FACES OF AGING

reality that in time even the most stubbornly youthful bodies move beyond the ideal image – and no amount of wonder creams or cosmetic surgery can change that.

The idealized image of the youthful body being the essence of strength and beauty is pervasive in our culture. But we are not only our bodies. We are at least as much spirit as we are bone and tissue. Some cultural traditions understand the material body as something to "overcome" lest it subjugate our spirit, as in many Buddhist teachings. If we adopt a touch of that attitude, we may be able to relax while all of those firm, youthful bodies jog down the path outside our window. We can strengthen our own "immaterial substance," meaning our minds and our spirits.

Imagine if we were not slaves to youthful images, or if we were truly proud of our wrinkles and embraced gray hair as a sign of the maturing process. Imagine if the less physically fit among us felt no less strong because of their perceived bodily shortcomings.

Different Kinds of Power

Our culture values a kind of power that is based on domination and possession. Quiet people are not seen as powerful, nor is the person who lets another person go first. The dominant model of power is patriarchal. It is based on "power over" rather than on "power to" or "power with." Patriarchal power disrespects the other ways we humans express power. The physically strong, the mentally quick, the verbally expressive are applauded, while the daydreamers, the playful, the patient and the sensual are denigrated. The former brand of power belongs more to the power of youth, the latter more to the power of *senex*, the elderly person.[12] We worship the power of youth even though we know it is only one of many different kinds of power.[13] By equating power with efficiency and growth and with speed and strength, we create unnecessary suffering in those who express their power differently. Temperaments and talents that stand in contrast to patriarchal power are devalued.

The elderly express their power in other ways than do the youthful majority. Their power is less based on physical power and more on a power that manifests itself through patience and service. This power is akin to what has been called servant leadership: "Laying emphasis on listening, acceptance and empathy, servant leadership functions in an introverted manner by means of interior connections, soul to soul."[14] The idea that power equals efficiency and growth may not serve us in the future. Environmental degradation, mounting dissatisfaction with the speed of life and ever-increasing disparities between the rich and poor suggest this. Perhaps we can glean from the elderly a different kind of power, one that does not negate our currently dominant one, but that acts as a balance to it by providing different possibilities. If we seek to move in this direction, we will gain an appreciation of the elderly's way of being and of their way of expressing power. We would see more closely just who they really are.

Imagine we were powerful because we were serving the needy. Imagine if we believed that behaving in a sensitive manner was a form of power, different from, but not less than, the power of domination and possession.

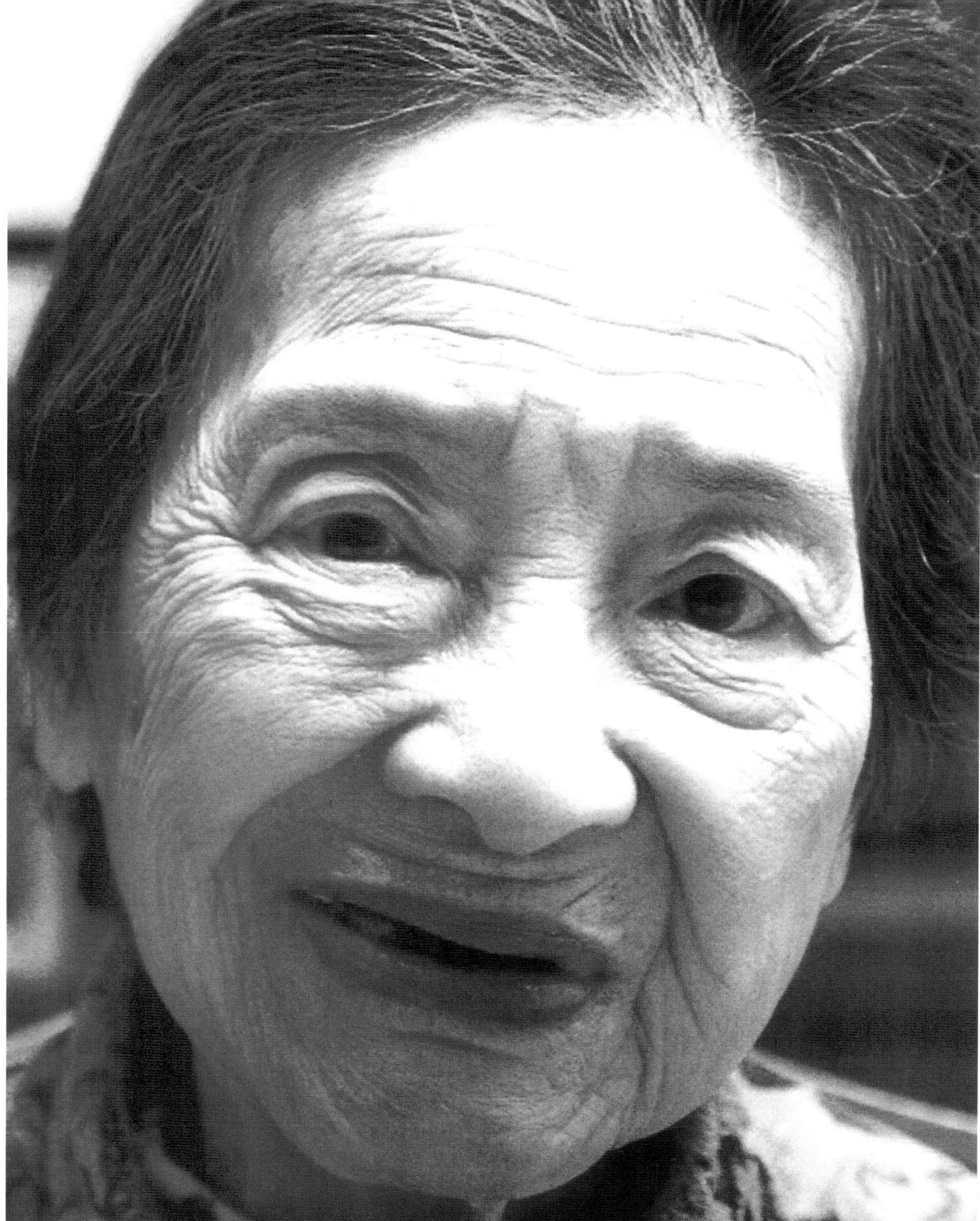

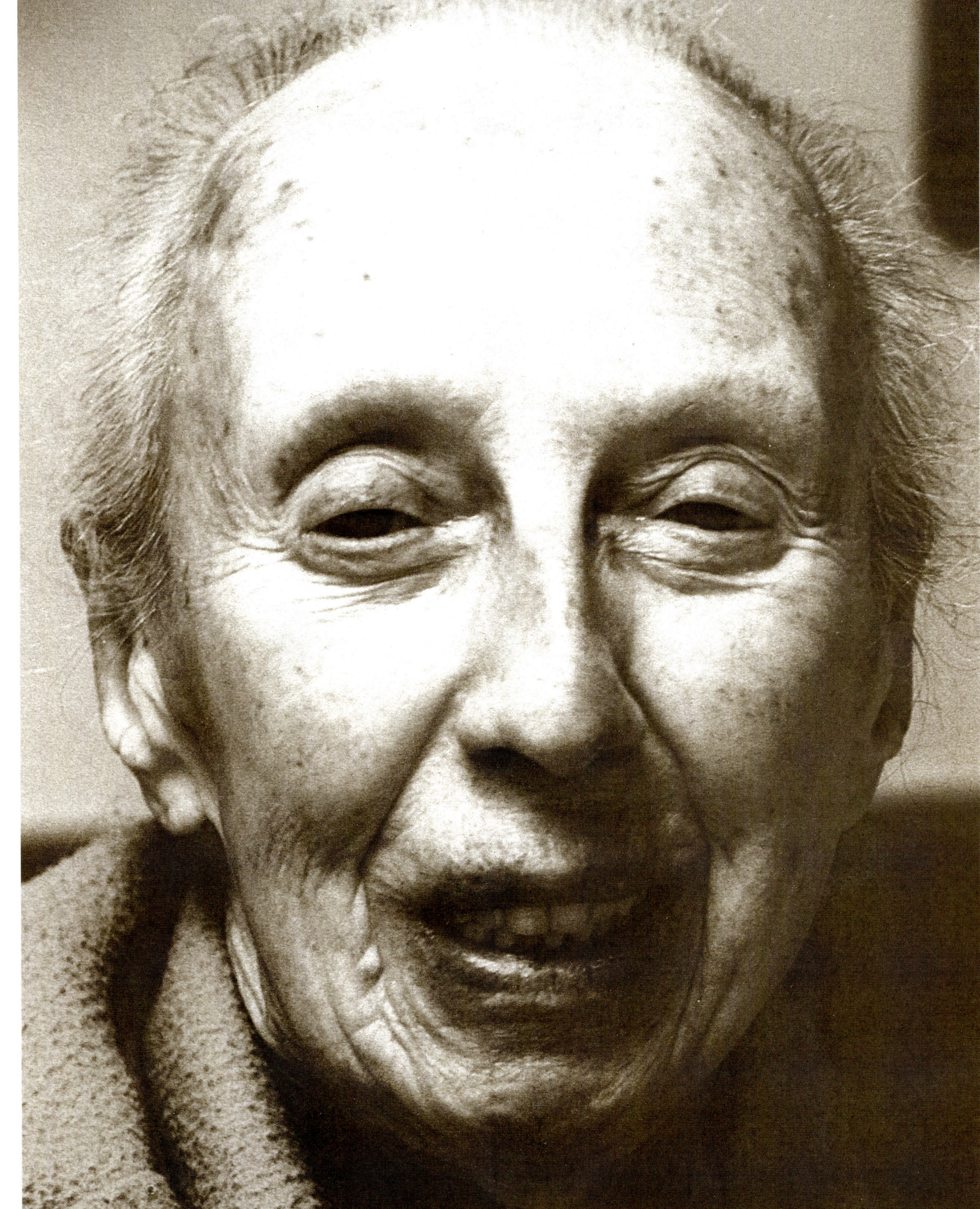

Elders and Sexuality

The elderly are as sexual as the youthful majority, and in some cases more so. This contradicts the common stereotype that older people are less sexual or even a-sexual. Mainstream culture seems to have an issue with grandpa and grandma getting it on. "Dirty old men" are those who evince sexual desires.[15] For women, derogatory terms such as "old hag" and "old biddy" stress sexual undesirability. We view sexuality as linked to power, virility and strength. Though such qualities ought not to be belittled, sexuality also involves lying next to your partner, holding and caressing. Our society has made a jump from sensuality to sexuality, and in the meantime we seem to have cut love and loving out of sexuality. Reports Benjamin Schlesinger: "[A] cardiologist was discussing some impending heart surgery with his patient, a 78-year-old woman. He asked her how often she and her 80-year-old husband made love, and she replied, 'Oh, we make love everyday.' The doctor was astonished! 'Do you mean you and your husband have sex everyday?' he asked. 'I think you misunderstand,' she answered. 'We have sex about once a week, but we make love every day.'"[16]

Our culture perpetuates the myth that older people are not sexually desirable, desirous or capable.[17] Worse, there is a sense of shame attached to older persons showing interest in sexuality. The severe distortion of sexuality as "characterized by passionate love-making and the achievement of sexual union through simultaneous orgasm," denies the elderly – as well as the rest of us – an important human expression.[17] This is so because the elderly will internalize these cultural ideas and feel ashamed to express their sexuality. They will deny themselves the pleasures and the sense of vitality that can derive from loving and being sexual.[19]

Imagine a shy and sensitive teenage girl learning that sexuality does not merely mean having "done it." Imagine her knowing that she is just as sexual if she is to "only" hold and be held by her boyfriend or girlfriend all night.

Going to Work

The issue of work is complex. The idea of meaningful work has eroded throughout the industrial age. For the majority of workers there may never have been meaningful work. As a result, the idea of retiring from an assembly-line job might be an attractive prospect. However, a university professor who loves her job might not want to retire. Maybe her work provides much of the meaning in her life.

Maybe it is time we redefine what we mean by work. Is work only work when it serves to help pay the bills? What if someone takes on some unpaid work? Is that still considered work? What if, for instance, a playground monitor looks after the children for free? Is that work? If I have fun working, am I really working? Hillman states this point succinctly as follows:

"Pleasure, like beauty and order, is one of the few great powers that move the cosmos. That the pleasure principle has been opposed to the work ethic degrades work into slavery and pleasure into childish truancies, causing us to regard pleasure as a decadent parasite sapping the strength of power."[20]

IF I HAVE FUN WORKING,

AM I REALLY WORKING?

I spent 19 days coming home from the Philippines. I couldn't fit into my bunk, which was against the ceiling, so I slept on deck the whole way home. I watched the porpoises, looked at the stars, and when it rained I got wet. They dropped us off on Angel Island, and I hitchhiked all the way to Oregon. When I was in the Philippines I don't think my wife knew where I was, because I never got a letter.

Floyd loves his treasure of fine ties
And tends them like a flower garden.
Wears them like a rose, for each of us.
To brighten our day.
A point of soft beauty in the pace of things.

Shuffles down the hall
Parsing out wisdom and wit,
Flashing a smile
And "Oh dear, and a bottle of beer."

His mood can thicken like soup.
A world turns, dark and furious.
Jousting the heavens, pounding on the door
Eye on the exit, fist on the floor.

FLOYD

This accurately suggests that people in their later years are often boxed-in in terms of opportunity for work because their motivations do not fit our attitudes toward who should work and why. My grandfather arose at 6 a.m. to feed and milk the cows every day of his adult life until he fell from a ladder at the age of 82. After he got out of the hospital he climbed right back up the ladder. He loved working. Telling him to stop would have been a death sentence. And nobody thought about telling him to stop, because for the farmers in his region it was understood that both men and women worked as long as they possibly could.

There is a lot of dormant potential among the elderly. Many would like to do something meaningful for themselves and for others, but, as Jack Rosenthal points out, "American attitudes toward retirement have never been simple. The justifications include a humane belief that retirees have earned their rest; or a bottom-line argument that employers need cheaper workers; or a theoretical contention that a healthy economy needs to make room for younger workers."[20]

At a recent conference on social issues, a young participant in his mid-twenties took up the microphone and said, "I don't understand. My grandfather is 91 years old, physically and emotionally still very fit, but he sits in his chair all day watching television. He has led such a rich life and has so much to give, so much to say." Sympathetic-sounding words, but it is not clear whether the grandfather was sitting in his chair all day out of choice or because he grew up within a culture that emphasizes the uselessness of the elderly.

It is not a pleasant picture – the image of someone sitting around all day watching television.

It feels wrong. It feels especially wrong if it happens because as a culture we have contributed to this state of affairs. One elder expressed this as follows: "Do not expect much help from us elders. Most of us have been relegated to retirement enclosures, golf, bingo, tourism, and uncreative play, separating ourselves from the problems of the homeless, the untaught, the unfed."[22]

This is sad. To live and work, feel and see, touch and think, experience and grow and then to be relegated to retirement enclosures in your later years, just when you should be most needed. A German newspaper headline recently summarized provocatively: "Contemptible to Retire Human Beings for Thirty Years." A life spent gathering so much experience and wisdom – is it not valuable for something? A. Stevens writes about the role that the elderly once played in the initiation of the young:

"Society at large has abdicated responsibility for initiating the young. Traditional initiatory procedures have been allowed to atrophy with disuse because our elders have lost confidence in the values of which they are the custodians and no longer possess any certain knowledge as to what it might be that they are initiating young people for. Ultimately, it is the fault of neither teacher nor pupil, elder nor novice, but the consequences of a collective crisis of confidence in our culture."[23]

It seems to me that we need the help of the elderly in whatever capacity they can and want to help us. Whether they are consultants, guides, teachers, or caretakers of the young, they have much to offer. Mining their resources would be a win-win situation, something that is good for them and good for us.

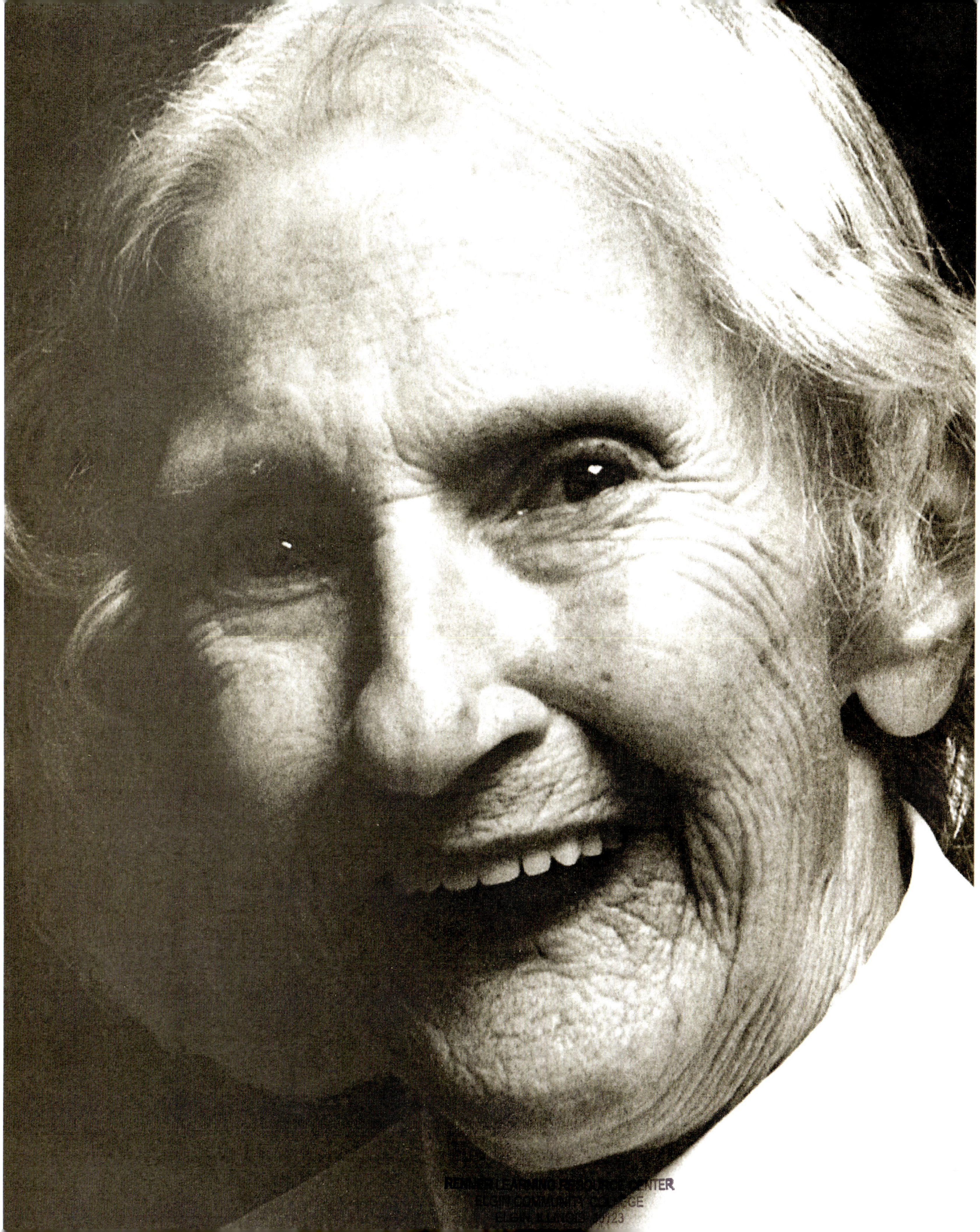

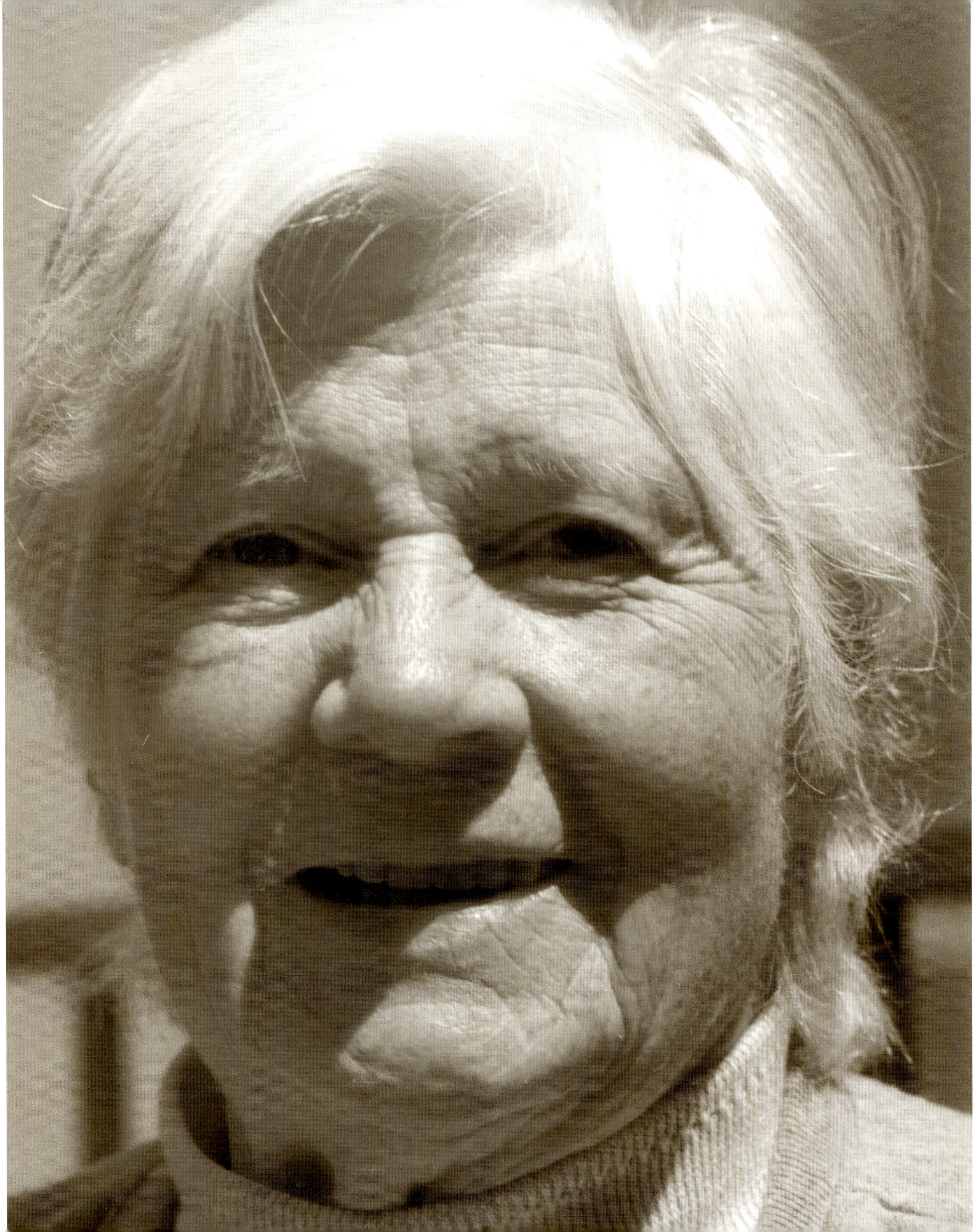

Imagine new, different images of work in society. Imagine evaluating your work – or yourself – not in terms of the amount of money you make but with the degree of fun involved in your work.

Doing What Really Matters

One cold winter day in Warsaw we stepped into a Vietnamese food bar for a bite to eat. While we were about to hand our plates back over the counter an old woman sitting next to us said shyly, "Excuse me, would you mind if I took your leftovers for some of the homeless dogs I feed?" We nodded, and she started to talk. She said she traveled to a remote district of Warsaw to buy cheap meat, often waiting at bus stops in the cold and the darkness, and then cooked and brought the food to stray-dogs in other parts of town. Her face shined as she spoke. We were moved, and she was grateful that we wanted to listen. She revealed that because of her care for the dogs, her sister and relatives considered her insane. They no longer spoke to her.

The story reminded me of something I read in Ram Dass' book *Still Here*: "In the face of our culture's dismissal of roles and activities that do not contribute to productivity, it is important that we be mindful of separating our values, as wise elders, from the values of those around us… most of us cannot expect kudos for participating in the sorts of activities that appeal to us in older age; there are no awards for planting gardens, or playing with our grandchildren, or taking stock of our lives; no social payback for practicing mindfulness, becoming conscious of our fears, unloosing the mental knots of a lifetime spent striving and achieving."[24]

Crazy Old People

Underneath that woman's weathered exterior lived a vivacious and "crazy-spirited" person who, like the rest of us, can be silly, playful, stupid, loud and childlike. But we see few of the elderly actually behaving this way. Why? The process at work is by now familiar: the majority in any society or culture creates a consensus reality and defines the things that are appropriate and the things that are not. Consensus reality tells us how to look at our world, tells us how to do the right things: the right fashions to wear, the right kinds of articles to buy, the right ways to behave. This has its advantages, but when consensus reality takes the form of stereotyping the elderly, the perceived right way can be hurtful. Imagine being given a dirty look when you giggle over a magazine headline in a bookstore? Or because you are humming a song you just heard on the radio?

Just like the process of pathologizing adolescent behavior as too hyperactive, socially deviant and rebellious – rather than understanding those behaviors as important indicators initiating an assessment of ourselves and society – we notice behavior that does not seem becoming of older people. The older the elderly get, the less they are noticed by the younger generations. If they do something that stands out, they become especially vulnerable to criticism. This can lead to the elderly behaving as if they are bound up in straitjackets. They need to constantly suppress their feelings, their joy and sadness about life, for fear that they will be mocked or derided. While not everyone might feel bad about being called "crazy" (indeed, plenty of young people relish such monikers), calling an older person crazy tends to carry a bite.[25]

Society's suppression of diversity and craziness is by no means limited to the elderly, but we tend to feel most upset when it is the elderly who are falling out of line. Indeed, some elderly delight in behavior that is deemed silly or childish. Such behavior is often a rebellion against age and the behavioral norms that society has imposed upon the elderly. As Hepworth points out, the "spirit of older people may well be much more resilient than is sometimes believed."[25]

Jenny Joseph expresses this "resilience of spirit" in her now famous poem "Warning." The poetess describes her desire to live free from the constraints placed upon us by ourselves and society when we are old. She wants to warn us about this slowly emerging desire so that "people who know me are not too shaken and surprised when suddenly I am old, and start to wear purple."

Imagine being old and cheerful in a "silly way" and the younger people around you laughing with you and being infected by your silliness. Imagine a teary-eyed teenager approaching you on the street and asking you for counsel in matters of the heart.

Caring and Time

It is hard to quantify how much the younger generations can learn from the elderly. They say that every generation has to make its own mistakes. But we do need to learn something that is very central to life: caring. The focus of our care is not the issue here. What matters is whether we can hold a caring attitude toward that which is around and in us. When I first began to ponder the concept of care, it seemed that the notion was not difficult to comprehend. In caring for the elderly, however, I find a deep complexity.

The two greatest elements in caring for the elderly involve time and presence. Despite their mundane surface meanings, these concepts are complex and difficult to explain. We all know full well when someone is giving their time and when someone is present with us. Children, in particular, sense whether an adult is truly there for them or whether that adult is rushed or between two things or busy with something else. While children are not shy about expressing disapproval when adults do not spend time with them, the elderly often do not express themselves when a caregiver appears to be "somewhere else."

Imagine being valued for merely sitting with someone, for giving your time to someone. Imagine that something like this is valued as much as the books you read, the degrees you have achieved, or the money you have saved. Imagine if men and women in corporate boardrooms were as concerned about a colleague's sick child as about the bottom line.

Time and Presence

Time and presence are linked. You cannot be present without time. You need time to be present. This is an important insight that bears repeating: you need time to be present. The essence of presence is time. To be present with an another being, you need to take your time.

A common phrase these days is, "I don't have time." This is a curious statement. It suggests that time is something to be had, like the money in our pockets or the clothes in our closets. But time is ever-present and intangible. We cannot live without it. To say we have no time is to say we are not alive anymore.

For example, at one time or another we have all become so absorbed in something that has made us lose track of time. We are surprised when we suddenly look at the clock and see how late it is. There is a link between being fully present with someone and forgetting about time. When we are unaware of time, we are truly present.

The notion of "forgetting about time" is central to the attitude behind care. When time is not pressing on our consciousness, we can be fully present. I remember a 40-year-old psychotherapy client who, after an initial eight months of belligerence toward me, suddenly began to sob bitterly during a session. After a long silence, I asked what had happened. He said he had just realized that no one had ever paid as much attention to him as I had during our work together.

Being with someone, giving him or her some time by being truly present, is a valuable gift. Especially in work with the elderly, giving undivided time is perhaps the deepest expression of our care for them. In turn, we are nourishing our own inner elder, learning to respect his or her ways.

Sadly, neither our culture nor our health-care system seem to support the notion that spending time is an expression of care.[27] Time must be spent "doing." Crudely put, if I do not *do*, I am wasting my time. If I do not *do*, I am not productive, or I am simply lazy. Time must be filled with doing. If you are not doing, you are thinking of doing something later. Maybe you are with a person, but you are thinking about being elsewhere. Time pressures override feelings. If I am conscious of time passing, my attention is divided and my feelings are divided. I am not really present with what is in front of me, with what is in me.

Our experience of time, how we use it, and how it uses us, stirs something in us. When we ponder time we ponder our meaning, wonder what it is we do with our life. Are we living the life we are meant to live? Or are we being led by social and cultural ideas of how we should live our life? We begin to wonder who is really in charge.

Remembering the vast spectrum of life as indicated by geological time – thousands and thousands of years of giving birth and of dying – might give us a certain sense of humility. And it might give us a feeling of relief by placing us within an immense universe of which we are an infinitesimally small yet vital part: relax, the world does not depend on you – eons have been, eons will be… .

Pondering time can bring us to wonder about what is important to be, important to do, important to live. It can bring us to wonder about the end of time, about dying, about death. "Taking time out of time nurtures that part of our being which is eternal," summarizes Ram Dass succinctly.

Imagine your eulogy. What do you want it to say? Your tombstone: what do you want it to read? Do you dare to live accordingly?

As an existential given, pondering time returns us to the essentials of life and our own life.

ARE WE LIVING THE LIFE WE ARE MEANT TO LIVE?

Long braids streaked with grey
wound up in coils or plaited down her curved back,
she sits with patient girlish delight. Sentinel of the wing backed chair,
handling the phones in a voice sanded by age but sweet as pie... "Hayes Valley Care"

– she sings out, responsible as an elder sister, serious, dutiful and glad.
I've seldom seen her sad, but when I have I've glimpsed her pain:
"it's my back, honey... hurts me all the time... ." Her arthritis is severe,
torturing her spine as the cruel string bends the bow.
I held her once on a picnic blanket in the park
among "sang-wiches" and cokes and rubbed her back
astonished by what she usually keeps inside
to show us such a happy face.

And just a day later she is able to play – and joins in songs –
loving the old ones best, "Red River Valley!" she calls out her request.
And lends her hearty voice to the blanket of sound.

This warms her and her friends. As does the magical tale of forty children –
living in San Rafael... and her quiet deference to this
her whereabouts must remain unknown.

Virgin and crone... Grandmother and girl,
She is an entire fairy tale
as are we all.
But in her eyes and in her smile it is truth. Each of us a fiction,
a child, a wise elder, and a poem.

MARY

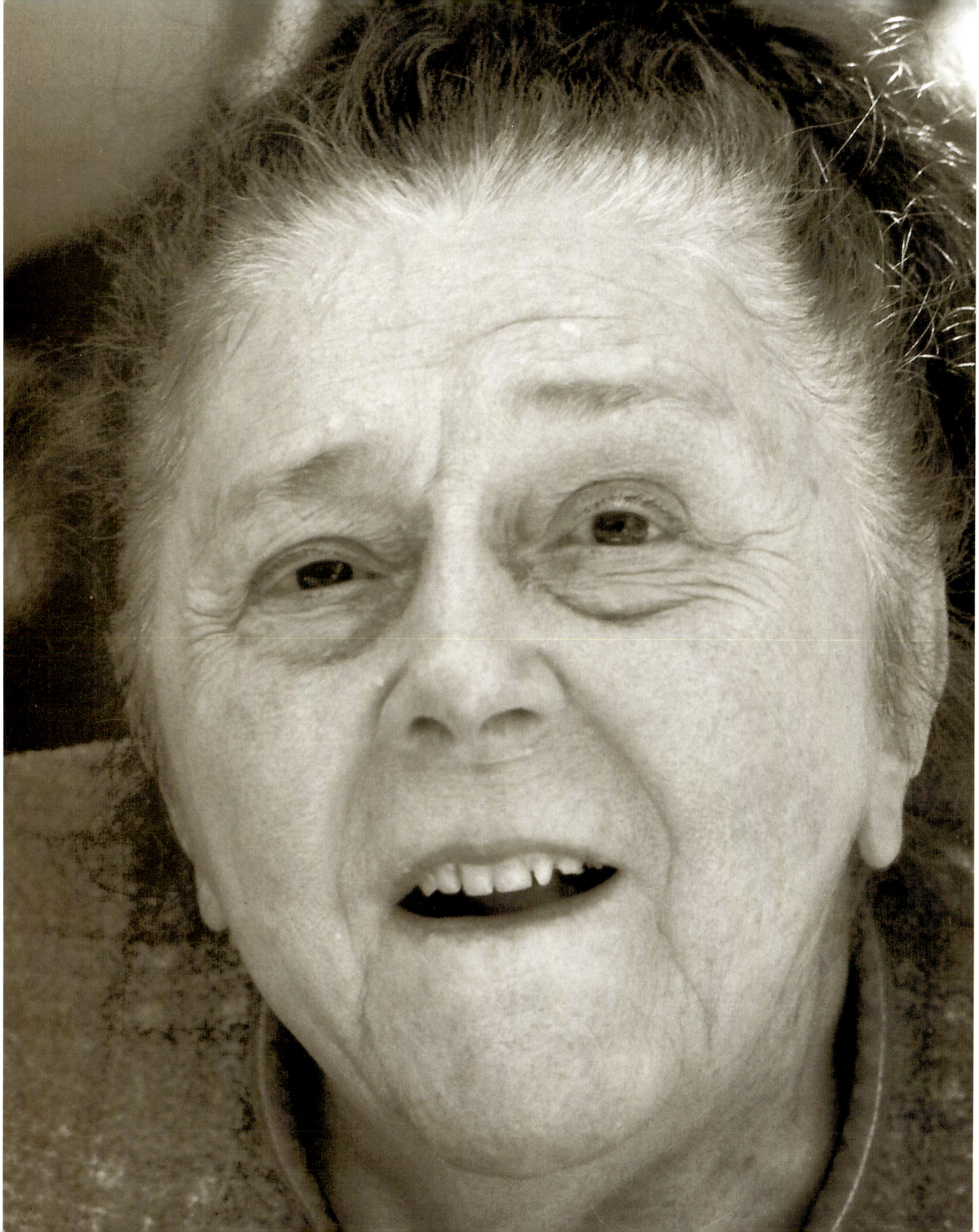

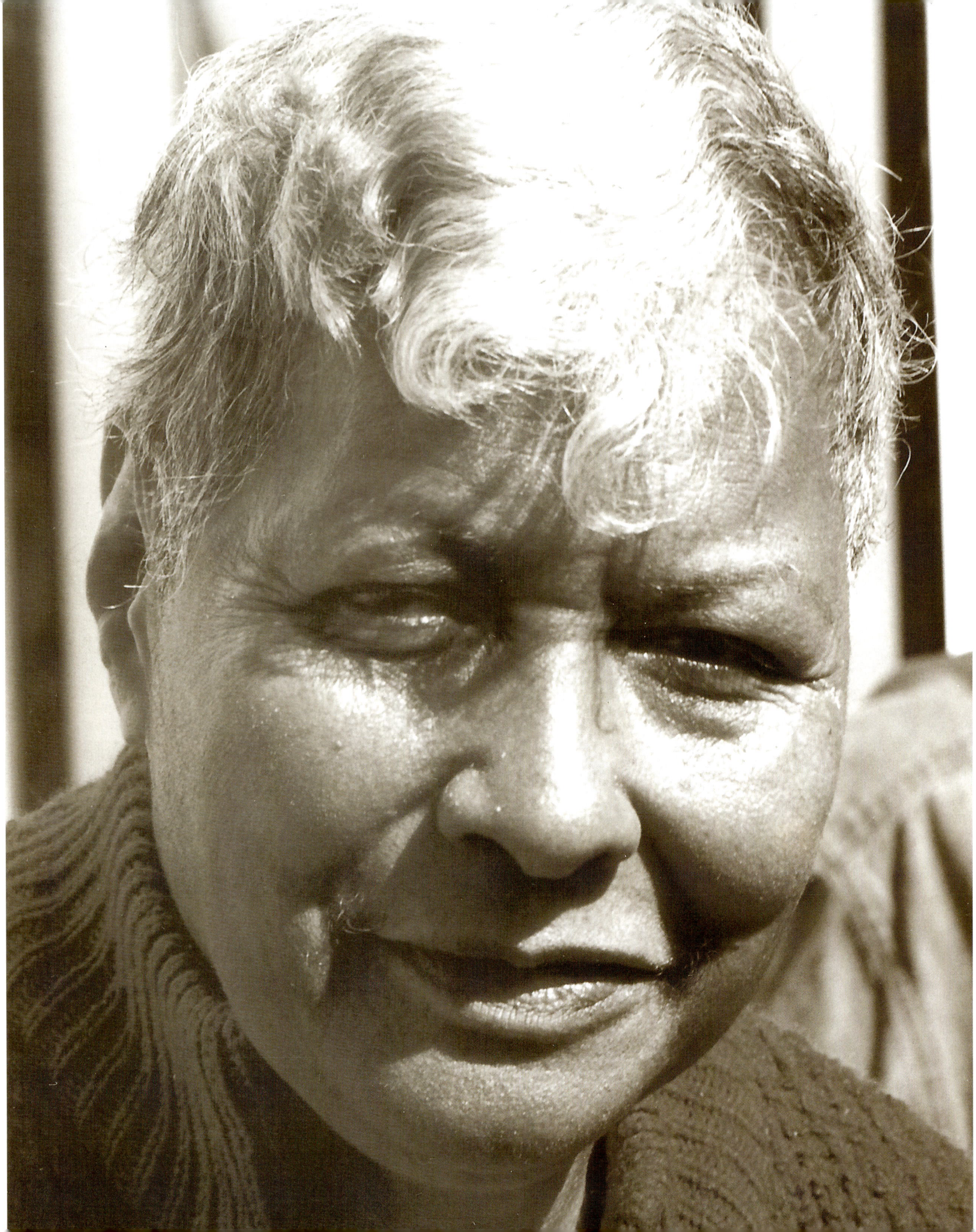

ALICE

Alice arrives at about eleven each day,
stepping through the door,
a soft amble of rhythm and blues
and purple, orange, and red,
sweaters and slacks bright and soft,
like her voice, spinning ribbons of gentle light in the hall.

She clutches a couple of purses and a newspaper,
things that help her hold the life she has known,
where knowledge and dignity cycled each day like the sun.

She holds her head high when she sings the old songs,
her voice warm, husky, yet high, with a touch of tremelo.
Just like she learned as a girl in her father's Baptist church.
We often share an easy joke. "Let the Church roll on!"
"Amen! Brother."

Fine hat festoons wide smile and dimpled cheeks,
sideways glance and downward flashing smile,
a little held back, then letting go, almost as an afterthought.
Studying her papers, today's news,
something to ground her words, which spin and float like dream images
held deep in the mind, part of a very wide field.

Patient, slow, and cautious, not quite ready to move,
not easily moved, perhaps in a minute, in her own time.
Ready to play and share her words
if she feels safe not to be shown
to be missing the moment, the meaning.

Strong, like a gentle old lion, sitting upright and regal,
Alice says she's satisfied, then mutters an aside,
some comment in code about what's happening in the group.

GEORGE

They call you Godfather
because of the way you smile
from beneath a fedora,
dismissive, one side of the lip curled
with irony at times…

Or is it because of the strength
of your grip? You sometimes steal a kiss,
bringing the back of my hand to your lips.

In the tumble of sand and honey
your voice mixes the lilts
of countries… Lebanon, Syria, Spain, Italy, and
here… you've had many an adventure
from a lonely start
a beautiful Persian wife and
handsome sons
punctuate the often tedious hours
of this present life.

Power still pulses in virile charm
unused to not having its way
forced to relent to the hurt in the body. The wily
orphan boy will out in your eye or
in the hushed awe of your voice
at the symphony when you leaned close to my ear,
stately, frozen legs warmed under tartan wool
to say, "all these people… so quiet… nobody talking…
imagine that!"

You are impressed by the power of the music
to bring us to another place.
You break your amazement like bread
and hand me a piece.

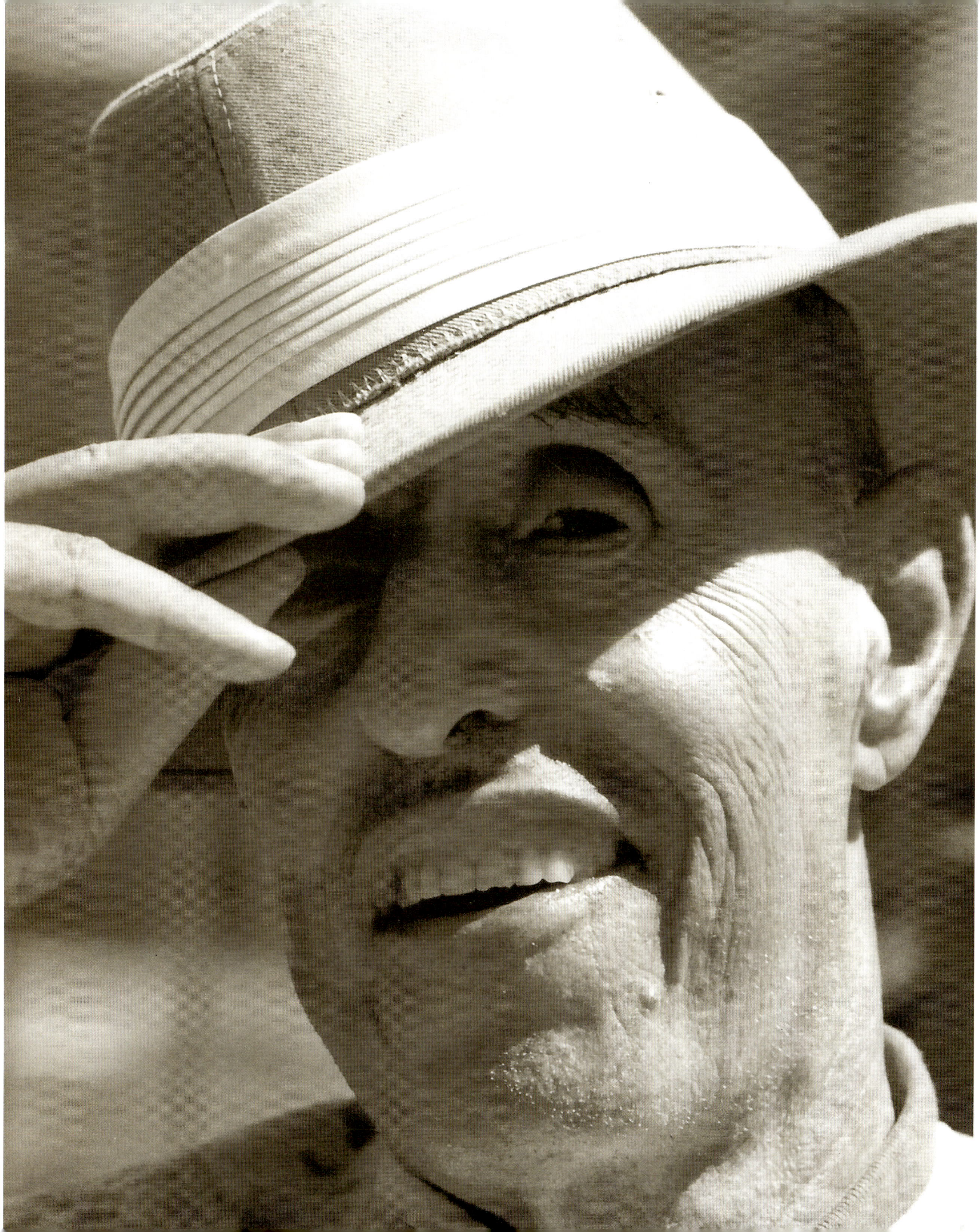

PART TWO • THE INNER ELDER

The idea of the inner elder holds that in each of us dwells an elder. Because this elder belongs to us alone, it is called our inner elder. To understand this, we have to first drop the prevalent belief that as humans we possess a monolithic identity. Consensus reality would like us to behave in a consistent and thus identifiable fashion; it does not appreciate it if we change our behavior from moment to moment. This doctrine of "one identity" is so strong that we do not recognize that we express different parts of ourselves at different times and under different circumstances.

For example, by paying attention, we may notice a different part of our personality when playing with children versus when fixing the vacuum cleaner in the garage. Or, when we are at work we behave differently than we do when we are in public. We might even give these different parts of ourselves certain names. We might call the part that deals with the public our social self. We can ascribe to it certain personality characteristics. For instance, the social self reveals fewer emotions than we might show our family and friends. It often speaks differently than the private self, appears more constrained in the way it reacts, is perhaps less impulsive or more measured.

Just as we can discern different kinds of personalities based on whether we are in a public setting or a private one, it follows that there are also different personalities based on our age.

This idea comes into focus when we realize, for example, that even though we are well past our adolescent years, we sometimes behave like teenagers when we are in a playful mood.

We might smile when we recognize ourselves in such a way, and depending on who we are with at the time, we can choose to accept or not accept that the adolescent in us is present. We often tease ourselves with comments such as, "You're acting like a baby," or "Don't behave like a teenager," or, more succinctly, "Grow up!" If we are paying attention, it's not hard to see that we can make contact with most of our different stages of life. We can also make contact with the person within us who we are still in the process of becoming. We know, for instance, that the seed of a tree grows into a mature tree. How does the tree itself know what it will become? It must already contain within its seed some knowledge of its final size, width, height, and so forth. Some of these characteristics will vary depending on environmental circumstances, on soil, wind, temperature, and so on, but the central point is that the seedling already "knows" what it will be like as a mature tree.

Humans are of course not trees, but when we are born there exists within us a potential that points the way toward the fully-grown mature adult that we will one day become. Whether we want to understand this potential as something inscribed in our DNA, or see it as our *daimon* (the ancient Greek word for human fate from which we derive the expression "the demon within us") – the fact is that there exists within us a purposeful intelligence that points to the fully grown mature adult within. Just as the tree needs sunlight and water, we need environmental support to grow to our potential. That is why everyday language is rife with expressions such as, "He needs to do something about his life," and "I wish she would live up to her potential." This potential is the fully-grown mature adult in us.

A GOAL IN OUR LIFE IS TO GROW INTO OUR INNER ELDER

But what does "fully-grown mature adult" really mean? It is important to clarify how consensus reality defines it. Mainstream society equates fully-grown mature persons with those among us who are anywhere from their mid-30s to late-50s, depending on the position of power they hold. If someone holds a very powerful position, this definition might even extend to later years (some U.S. presidents are prime examples of this). Exceptions aside, however, society defines fully mature people as those people who are in their middle years, not in their later or older years.

As described before, this definition is based on stereotypical attitudes of strength, whether muscular, intellectual, or both. From the point of view of physical strength, a farmer would be strongest between his 20s and his 50s, but in terms of knowing and sensing the best times to sow or reap, older farmers carry more experience and knowledge (and can usually expect their children to consult them on such matters).

In terms of wit or intellectual agility, a trait much valued in our society, we have to remember that intellectual knowledge is only one way of knowing the world. As Lakritz points out, in "our American culture we have overemphasized the intellect, trusting it to guide our whole human conduct. We mistrust and devalue the intuitive wisdom of our hearts."[28]

And in terms of intuitive wisdom or depth of understanding, it is not the thirty, forty or fifty-year old who is fully grown and mature; it is the old person, the elder, who has learned something about wisdom, about the richness and complexity of life.

Given this redefinition of the fully-grown mature adult, the intelligence that is contained within us, whether DNA, daimon or destiny, understands its goal of unfolding as the last, not the middle phase of life.

C. G. Jung and other thinkers have pointed out that the goal of life is death. Maybe we should tweak that assertion by adding that before we die the goal of our conscious life is to grow into our inner elder. If so, we can leave our earthly existence in as conscious a fashion as possible. This, in turn, would mean that the goal of life is to become as aware as possible.

Again, this awareness finds its culmination in the form of our inner elder.

The Inner Elder as Guide

The assertion that each of us has an inner elder carries with it several implications. The main inference is that we can find a way to make contact with this inner elder. Doing that would give us a powerful ally as we travel through life. In times of decision making, of needing to choose a path, our inner elder might provide invaluable counsel. It might not provide specifics regarding individual decisions, but it might remind us of the larger framework enclosing those decisions. It might tell us how a decision will further or hinder us from becoming who we are.

Secondly, once we are aware of our inner elder, we start to see the elders outside of us (the other older people in our community) in new and different ways. We might feel more appreciative of what they have to offer, and we might become more interested in their

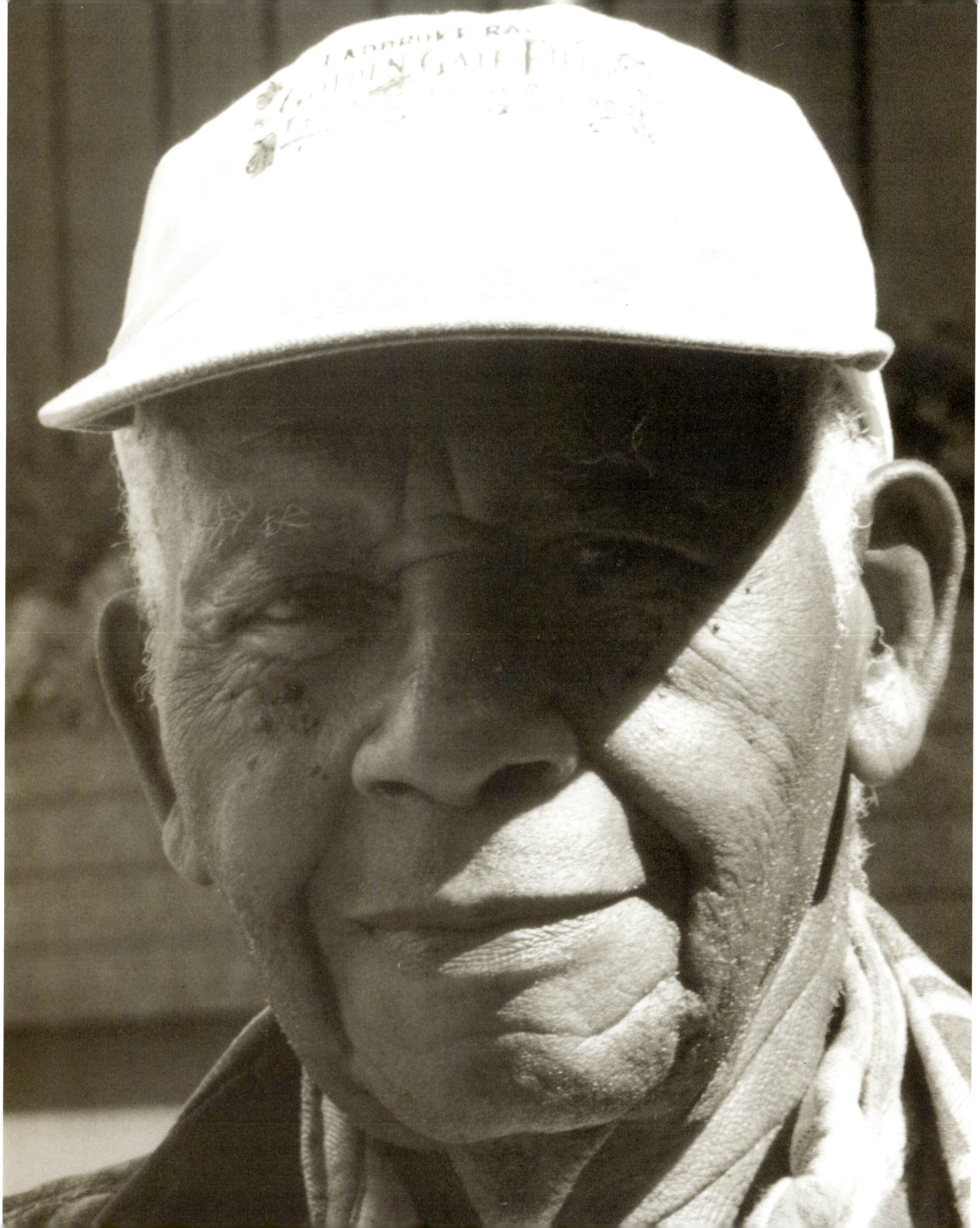

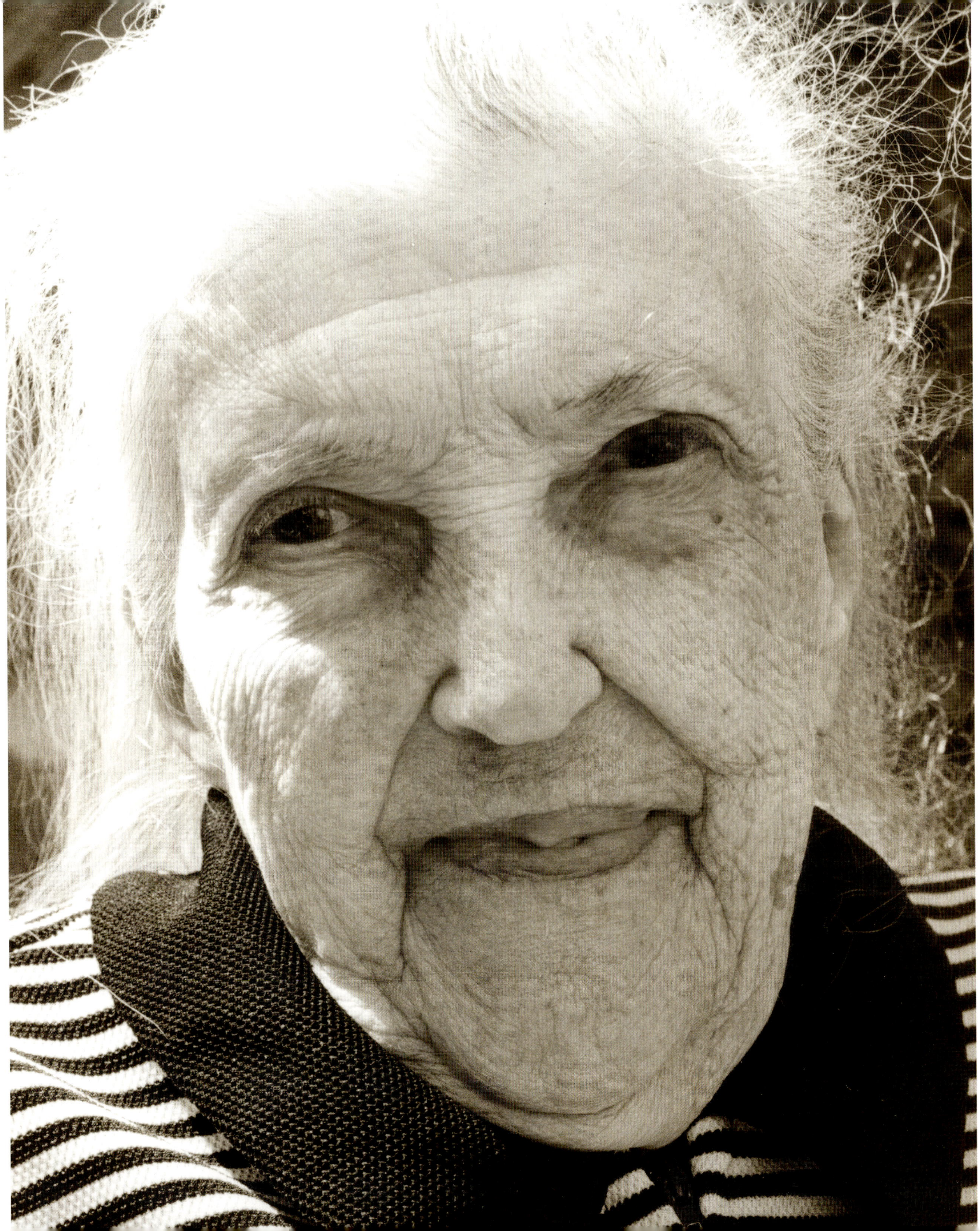

experiences and in the ways in which they have lived their lives.

Thirdly, we start to see our own lives from a larger perspective. "Live long by looking long," Lao Tzu reminds us.[29] When we get caught in the minutiae of day-to-day details, when we are ensnared by the small stuff, we have someone who can bring us back to our center, to the things that truly matter in our lives, we have help in evaluating what is important and what is not. We learn to look at life and its components from a distance, from a more detached position. We learn to see ourselves as less central.

Making Contact with Your Inner Elder

I am reminded here of a five-week training program that I attended some years ago. The large group of participants included people from 27 countries. Some time during the fourth week of the workshop, the group suddenly heard an unfamiliar voice.

A Japanese woman of slight built had ever-so-quietly begun to say a few words as the group gathered for its usual end-of-day session. None of us participants had heard this voice in the group before, and indeed were so surprised to hear it now that we strained to catch every word she said. When she finished talking, the room was deathly silent. Finally someone asked softly why she had not spoken earlier. She answered that she had not known how. To her, everyone in the workshop was quick, spoke loudly and fluently, and knew what to say. She said that she had no well-formulated sentences prepared, that English, not her first language, caused her some shyness, and that she knew her voice was soft and she felt no one would hear her. She felt there had been no space within which to speak. She felt intimidated, out of place.

By the same token, when we consider wanting to make contact with our inner elder, we might remember how hard it is to listen to a quiet voice that is not accustomed to speaking, especially when everyone else speaks with volume and vigor and is able to grab attention.

This is the situation of the inner elder. He or she has been quiet for a while, has not been recognized as an ally. In addition, our own inner elders might have experienced different forms of mistreatment. This mistreatment might find overt expression in the way we become upset with older people who are slow or otherwise in our way, or it might take the form of us ignoring the elderly people we meet, of not making them feel needed or important as members of our community of friends, neighbors and associates. This disregard and neglect is hurtful to the elder within. Hillman points out that any impatience or insult we level against "elders without" affects the elder within in the same way.

Reluctance to speak, fear of expressing oneself, or fear of not being heard in today's society can suppress the wisdom of the inner elder.

Our unconscious ways of marginalizing the elderly *and* our own inner elder continue to perpetuate this fear.

Saying Hello

It is necessary to proceed with sensitivity and care when making contact with our inner elder. Above all, we need to take our time and create space. We need to make the encounter with our own elder a priority, not something that we squeeze between a few other appointments. We can start with a "life review," let ourselves hear where we currently are in life, how we feel at the moment about the things that we do.

Then we might start to imagine what it would feel like if we were old. There is no need to choose an exact age here, just an image of old age, what we consider to be old. As we "feel into" this figure, we might want to pay attention to how comfortable we are with him or her, take some time to explore this old person who is us. Once we feel familiar with our inner elder, we might ask if he or she has a name; we might ask some questions about feelings and opinions.

Going Deeper

At first, you might or might not go much further than saying hello to your inner elder. If you soon feel comfortable around him or her, you might want to go more deeply into understanding the elder. That might mean asking questions that strive to learn more about what is important to the elder (you) now that he or she is an older person. How does he or she spend time now? What is meaningful at this stage of life?

Another aspect of growing into one's inner elder involves inviting questions, responses or commentary on the way you are living your life now and on how this life appears to your inner elder. You might want to ask if there are things your elder would want to change in the way you live your younger years, or if there are things that make sense or do not make sense when looked upon from afar. By doing this, in many ways you would be asking for guidance in times of stress or if you feel lost or unsure.

Walking in Your Footsteps

As we become more familiar with our inner elder, we start to take more notice of the older people around us. We become interested in the way they walk, talk, the speed at which they move, the things they do and say. We might want to engage them in conversation, whether in a café, at a supermarket, or on the street while waiting for a streetlight. When we do this, we start to see the richness of life, the infinite variety of stories and ways of living a life from a fresh perspective. And we begin to understand something about our journey, become aware of the ups and downs, the small things and the big stuff. We start to feel more confident about our own journey as we hear the variety of journeys lived. We slow down a little, start to incorporate the depth in which our inner elder moves. At times we notice that the smaller disasters in life, the car getting dinged, the bank account going dry, do not upset us as much as they used to. After all, from the perspective of the elder, of a life lived, how much impact do these things have on life? How devastating can they truly be?

Stepping Back: The Long View

Perhaps the most important lesson that an inner elder can teach you is this ability to step back from your life and take the long view.

The events that transpire, the feelings you feel, the tasks of the past, present and future, are all relativized when you take the long view. Just as significantly, you start to question whether you are presently – now – in some way furthering this long view of your life. You wonder whether what you are currently engaged in is of meaning given the larger purpose(s) in your life.

The Big Questions

What if all we needed was to sit still? What if there was nothing to do, only something to be? What if we could wield as much influence on the world by being still and working on ourselves as we would by running around? What if we had no possessions yet felt provided for? Imagine everyone sharing all the wealth? What if we were powerful beyond belief? What if in giving we received? What if we became a mystic? A wealthy business-person? A poet? A pop-star? A saint? A philosopher?

From the perspective of the elder, these are the big questions that we start to ask about life and living.

Personal and Larger Concerns

Big questions allow us to see our own lives in a larger context. Rather than feeling like isolated individuals, we understand that we are part of a larger home comprised of the community of us humans interconnected with our planet.

We understand that we are as much spiritual beings as we are physical beings. As such, we appreciate and respect the diversity of life and want to do all we can to protect it. Our inner elder informs us even at a young age of the importance of moving beyond our own selves and being concerned about the world around us. We would not harm others for short-term selfish gains because we would be harming ourselves. Because our inner elder knows that life has its own ways of guiding us, we are less afraid of not being in control of things. Through the elder we have a way of knowing that everything will turn out the way it needs to turn out. We can accept the vicissitudes of life and know that any excessive preoccupation with material things will not benefit our growth in the long view.

You're Not Old Until You're Ninety[30]

The challenges we confront in old age are different than those of middle age, and not only because physical strength and the intellect might be waning. It is more to the point to say that we demand different things from ourselves when we are in our older years. We are no longer content to swim the waters that we swam in our earlier years. The challenges are now those of depth, of deepening our awareness to understand the sheer and infinite complexity of life.

And then there is the challenge of learning and knowing how to use our life experiences and place them at the service of the generations that come after us, of guiding them gently and compassionately.

This, perhaps, is one of the most difficult tasks awaiting us in our older years: How can we learn not to insist on what we know, but to remain open to the changes that must occur? How can we guide without leading, or care without lessening the trials and tribulations that are necessary to everyone's growth?

> **HOW CAN WE LEARN NOT TO INSIST ON WHAT WE KNOW?**

*A sharp laugh always catches me
unawares, napping in my life, used to its pulse
until the wave of his delight breaks upon my ears.
He loves to read – all day sometimes.*

*I've wondered about his world, as rich and distant at times
as his national geographic underwater whales. When I ask him,
"Mr. Ray how are you?" He waits a moment before answering...
"... fine..."
And I realize that he has been sensing himself,
going inside,
to find out how he really feels.*

*He yelled at me once. I interrupted his nap
to ask him to do crafts,
and he told me, with force, that he was tired,
and wanted to go lie down.*

*The next day I thought he might not recognize me, and just walk by...
but instead he took my hand in his own,
warm and brown, and said, "... I would like to apologize..."
He told me "I was very angry..." and "... I'm sorry."
And he cried.
He said, "you have always been kind to me."*

*And we hugged. And then that silence.
He strode off with his teddy-bear's gait, turned,
looked back, and said
"... thank you."
Once we walked on water,
picking our way together over flat and narrow stones after sipping Japanese tea...
We danced.*

*We stood together on what he called "a perfect day"
and watched the seals on spits of sand braying to their pups.
He confided to me... "every book I read, I think is the best book I've ever read...
but one book in particular...
really opened me up..."*

*And I knew that though injured, his mind is clear –
different perhaps than mine –
but much the same, too...
sharing one friendship with me
which both of us can name.*

JAMES

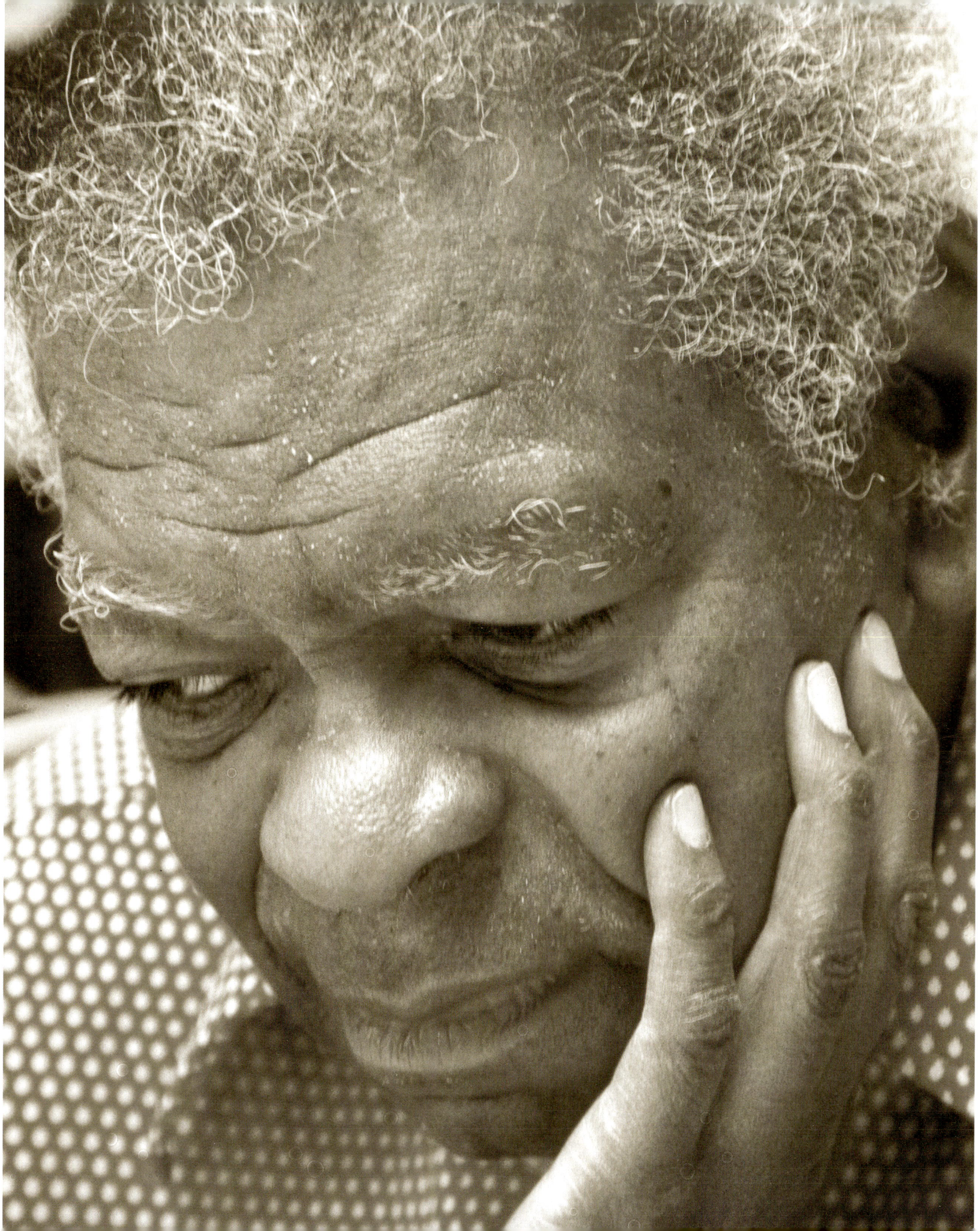

ETHEL

Slender as a young heron
she is not a child, but child-like at times,
fierce blue eyes softened by a commander's kindness
she can afford to be generous, and offers me her phone.

"It's in my room she assures me confidently;
"you may use it if you wish,"
and nods. And that is all for now.

I've seen her weep for her mother and tell me that she'll see her soon.
"She is very near now."

I ask if she will see father, too...
"Oh no," says she... "He lives below,"
and both eyebrows arch is if to say
"– you know...?"

A butterfly adorns translucent hair, like opal,
once blonde. She sniffs freshly arranged flowers and her mouth curls broadly with delight.
She leans in close and whispers with emphasis, "we girls have to do these things together
with all these men around."
The room is filled with women now, but long ago she was alone,
a bold young girl-officer,
saluted and even feared.
Today she still will say "at ease,"
if asked to, with pride.
And what comfort I have felt in hearing her.

Like a silver rapier her body cuts suddenly through space
or mincing gingerly along through Symphony Hall behind a walker,
on her young attendant's arm
all eyes turn upon her beauty, so certainly old
and delicate yet strangely strong.
Breath is drawn
as many lives stop for a moment and remember that
we are all passengers of time.

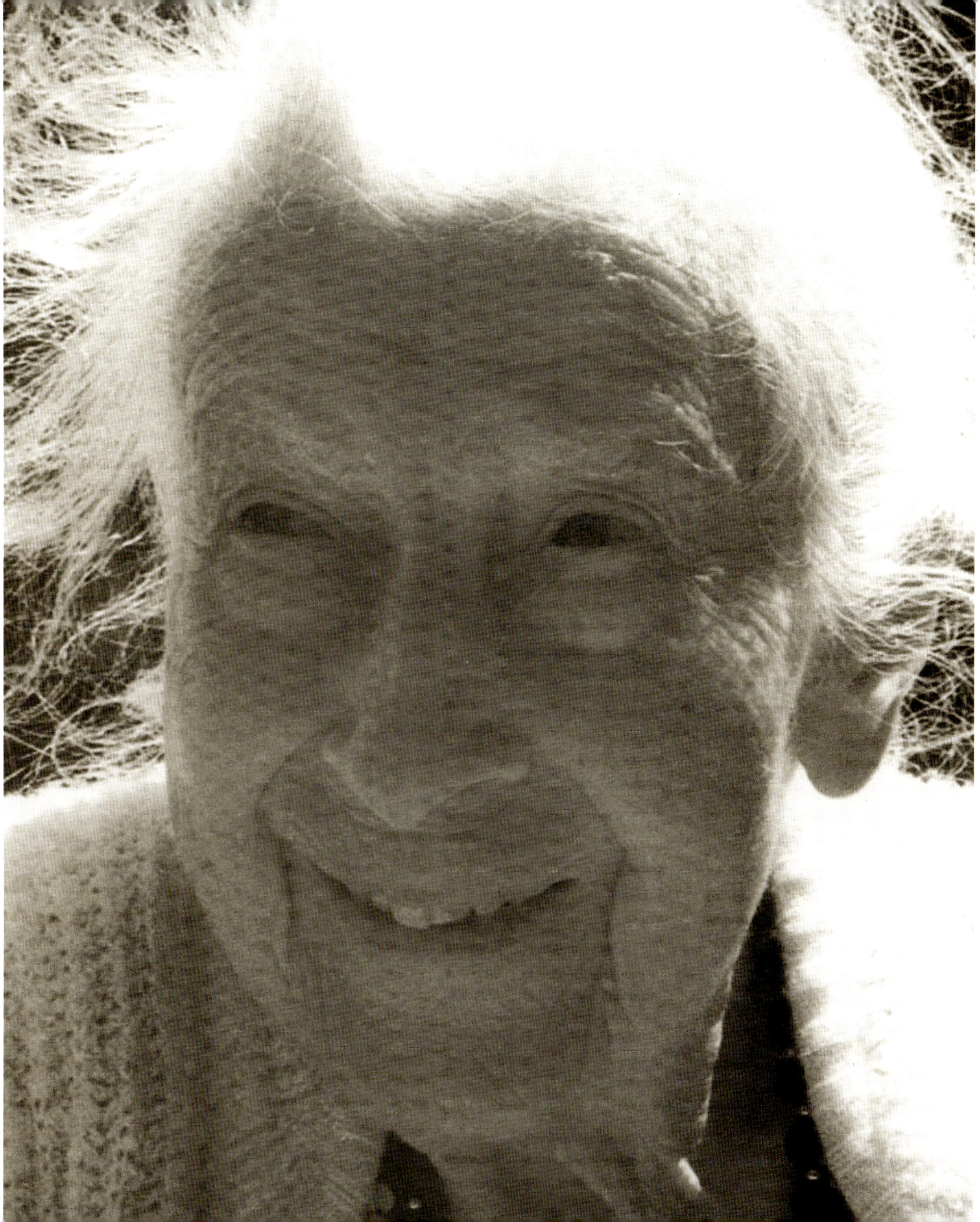

PART THREE • ON BECOMING AN ELDER

Who is an Elder?

In an interview entitled *Calling all Elders*, Michael Mead emphasizes that "aging does not make an elder. Age makes us older. It is a matter of what a person has learned while aging. Elders, by tribal imagination, and more recent definition, are those who have learned from their own lives, those who have extracted a knowledge of themselves and the world from their own lives. We know that a person can age and still be very infantile. This happens when the person does not open and understand the nature of his or her own life and the kind of surprising spirit that inhabits him or her."[31]

I understand elders as those people who have reached a certain distance from who they are. This means they are concerned not just with their own personal lives, but also with social and planetary concerns. They have experienced the cyclical nature of life and understand something about what is and is not important from the perspective of a life lived. Elders do not get ensnared in the latest trends and fashions or the latest news, because they have seen how these things are only waves that come and go. In matters of the heart, they have learned first hand of love and pain, of passion and desire, of anger and attachment. Having experienced these emotions and states of being, elders know they have no answers.

They also know that life is more a matter of living with questions than of living in certainty. Elders know about the impermanence of matter and the importance of mind and spirit, of learning to control the senses. They know of the limitations of human reason and intellect and the importance of an open heart. Elders have a different sense of time than younger people do. They have learned through experience that everything takes time. They know that things cannot be rushed before they are ready and know – especially – that the timing of the human heart remains enigmatic.

Elders conserve and are respectful of all that exists, because they know of the preciousness of all life, whether organic or inorganic. They understand that every decision is complex and has multiple and unforeseen effects. Elders are wise because they have traveled through life, have made mistakes, have seen the patterns of life.

To be an elder is to take on a role, a certain attitude toward life and towards the present moment. As such, to be an elder is to be free from chronological time, to be attached to the eternal wisdom coming from the heart. An elder is aware of the process that is unfolding right before his or her eyes and is detached enough to see the patterns and structures of events, and yet remain in awe of the mystery of life.

According to Arnold Mindell, the role of the elder differs from the role of the leader in various respects:

"The leader follows *Robert's Rules of Order*, the elder obeys the spirit. The leader seeks majority, the elder stands for everyone… . Leaders try to be wise, elders have no minds of their own. They follow the events of nature… . The leader knows, the elder learns."[32]

There is a growing interest in eldership among feminist writers and the men's awareness movement started by people such as the poet Robert Bly, psychologist Michael Mead, and many others. In discussing Russian fairy-tales, an anonymous writer wrote:

"The older woman is the keeper of wisdom and tradition in her family, clan, tribe and community. She is the keeper of relations, whether they be interpersonal or with all nature. Every issue is an issue of relationship. It is assumed she has a deep understanding of the world's great mysteries, birth and death.

Another quality is the ability to be mediator between the world of spirit and earth. She is emancipated from traditional female roles of mothering and is free to make a commitment to the greater community. As a result of this freedom, there is an abundance of creativity unleashed in this phase of life, often expressed through art, poetry, song, dance, and crafts, and through her sexuality as she celebrates her joy."[33]

We need to understand more of who the elder is. The concept should be discussed, reflected upon, filled with various experiences, expectations and dreams. Looking back to tradition and forward to the future, we need to keep searching for the meaning of this word so that it can guide us in our late as well as in our early years of life.

Awareness

The most important tool we have on our way to becoming an elder is awareness.

"Aging consciously, we will naturally begin to manifest those qualities that our society needs in order to survive, qualities of sustainability, justice, patience and reflections. These qualities can only come from the space of Awareness which age invites us to explore," writes Ram Dass.[34]

Be Prepared

It has been said that "the trouble with old age is that no one is interested in it until they get there." But again, there is a difference between being old and being an elder. The former you cannot avoid, the latter requires preparation. This means that we have to be interested in old age before we reach it.

To develop the traits necessary to grow into an elder, we need to practice being an elder. The subtitle of Rebecca Latimer's book *You're Not Old Until You're Ninety*, states this succinctly: "Best To Be Prepared, However." She describes the journey from her fifties to her nineties, a time during which she "had been gradually led to this happy place where I can handle my problems and enjoy my old age."[35]

With average life expectancy now reaching into the late seventies, being old is no longer the luck of a few. Old age has become a reality with its own demands. Just as we use our youth to prepare for the demands of adulthood, to prepare for careers and economic security and something meaningful with which to occupy ourselves, in adulthood we should begin to prepare for our later years. Such preparation so far has been almost exclusively limited to ensuring our financial well-being in the form of pensions and other such monetary preparations. That is not enough, however, if we want to live a meaningful life beyond our middle adult years.

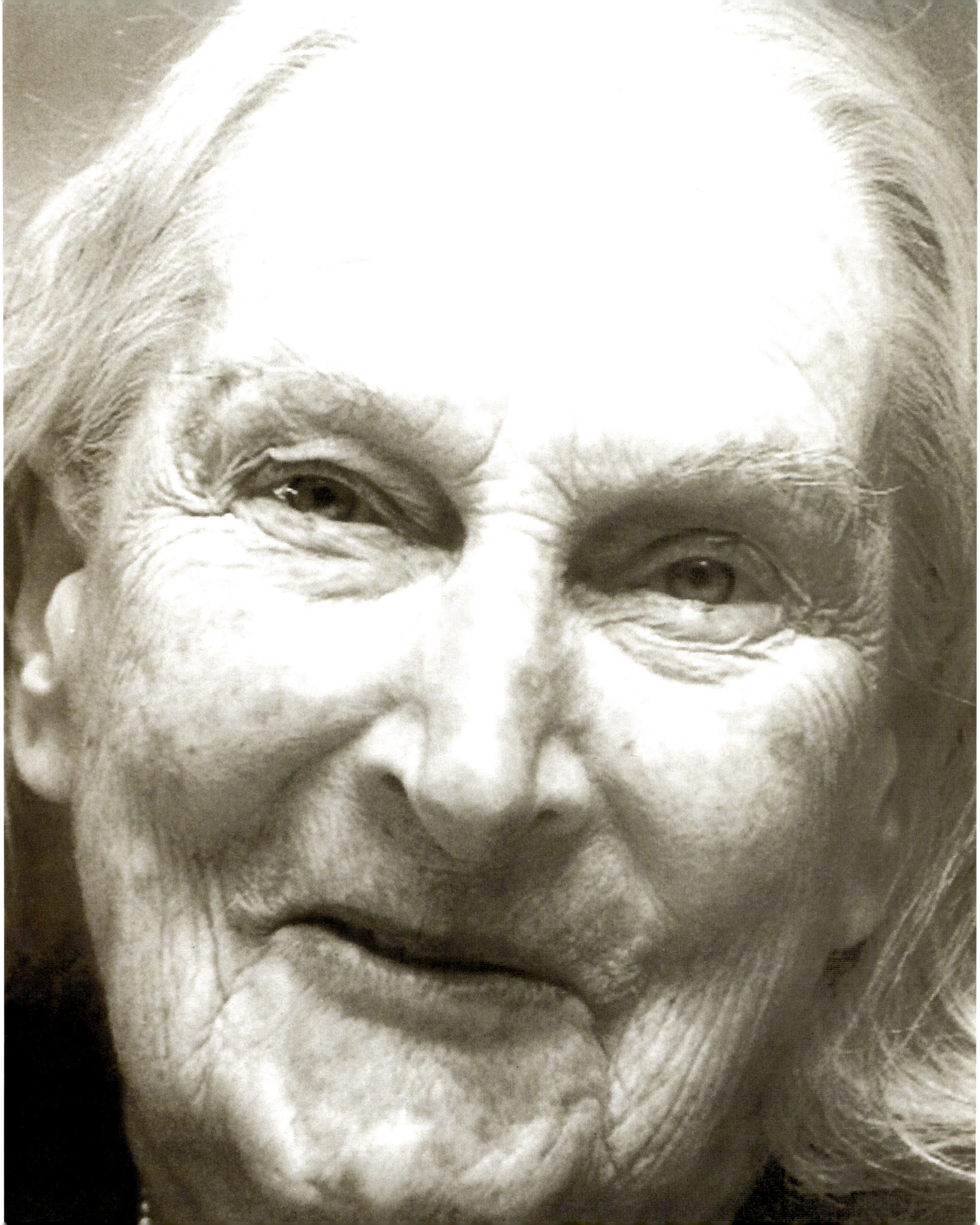

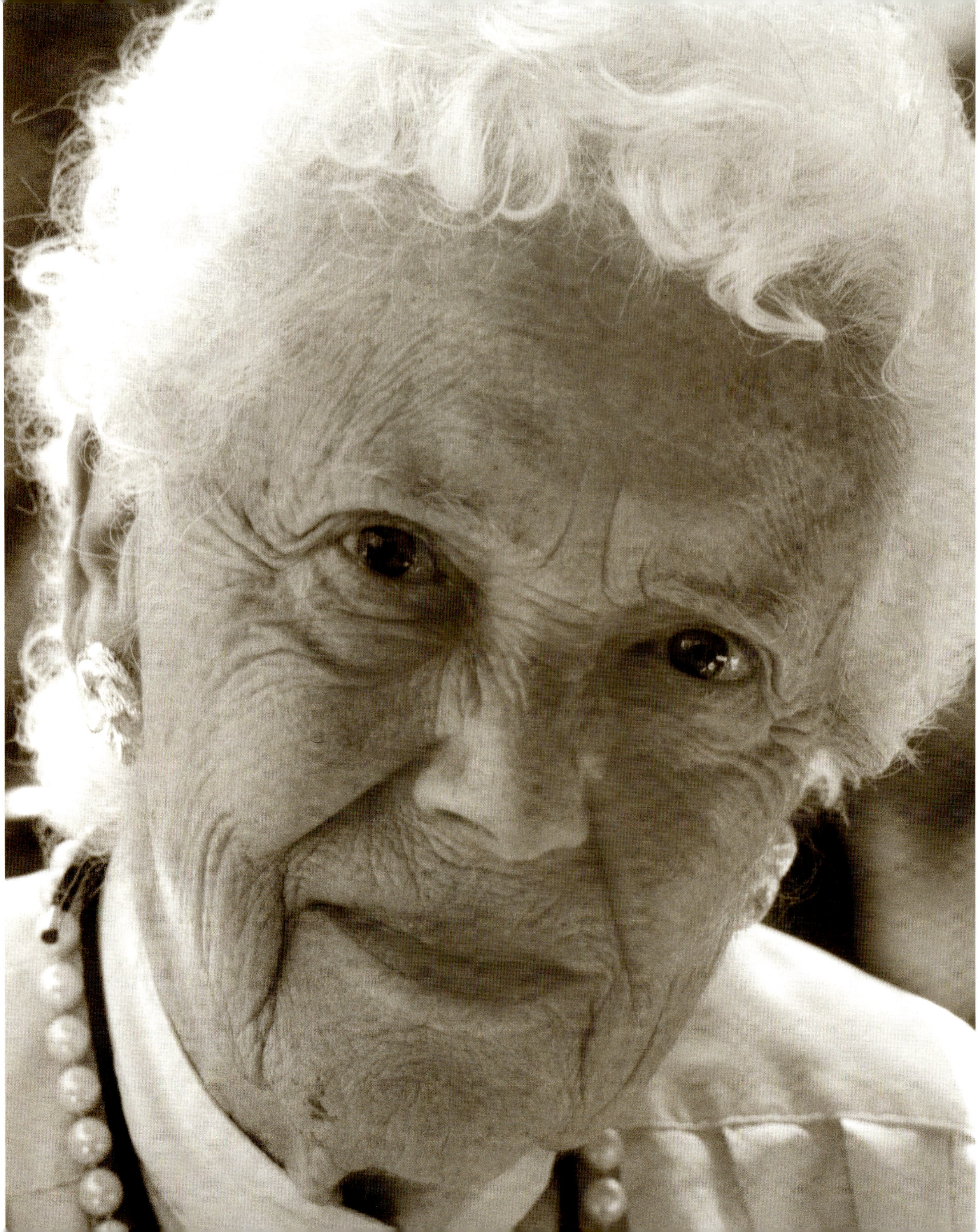

Waking-Up

How would we like to be when we grow older? What plagues us? What constitutes an elder? Not everyone wants to be an elder or wants to expend energy in becoming one. Again, becoming an elder takes preparation, which in turn equals effort. And effort takes time away from other priorities in life. Becoming an elder takes commitment.

It bears repeating that making a commitment to a continual journey of learning and understanding, of gaining awareness, of becoming an elder – doing this is as much a personal journey as it is a hope for the elders in our community.

At 92 years, Latimer expresses this as follows: "The way I see it, the first rule is to be open to new ideas, to be non-judgmental. Don't ask the younger generation to follow the rules you learned so many years ago. Any change is hard to accept as you grow older… ."

And she summarizes our choice: "It is much easier to cling to your past values, to judge everybody and everything by the standards you have always trusted, but if you do, you will be left on the sidelines. The future will pass you by, and you will be sitting in your rocking chair, grumbling and complaining with all the other old codgers."[36]

If we hope to become an elder, we are expressing a desire to keep learning, to continue to challenge our ways of thinking and to fuel our desire to be involved in something larger, something beyond ourselves. We want to understand what we have to do to prepare for our latter years, for giving ourselves in a way that can be accepted, is useful, and can be heard.

We can find inspiration through people we have found to be genuine. These people exemplify characteristics we admire. They do not seem invested in whether or not their listeners become a convert to what they say, do not seem to be driven by egotistical needs of recognition or by an interest to convince, shine, or stand out. They exude a certain selflessness, a noticeable humility and down-to-earth-ness.[37]

Not Just One Way

"There is no right or wrong way of getting old," Ram Dass points out. He continues: "A great source of suffering in our culture, and one which hounds many people as they age, is that if they could just figure out how to do things right, there would be no suffering in age. If they could just learn to succeed in aging correctly."

A lack of pattern may also be a blessing, a kind of wisdom in itself. There are as many ways of being old as there are people. The point is to embrace the uniqueness, all of who you are, and share it with those who are around you.

WHAT DOES IT TAKE TO BECOME AN ELDER?

FACES OF AGING

Being Less Perfect

The following thoughts are those of an eighty-five-year-old man who learned that he was dying. These reflections show something about "looking long", about seeing life from a "mature" perspective:

"If I had my life to live over again, I'd try to make more mistakes next time.

I wouldn't try to be so perfect.

We all have perfection fetishes. What difference does it make if you let people know that you are imperfect. They can identify with you then.
Nobody can identify with perfection.

I'd relax more. I'd limber up. I'd be sillier than I have been on this trip. In fact, I know very few things I'd take so seriously.

I'd be crazier. I'd be less hygienic. I'd take more chances. I'd take more trips. I'd climb more mountains. I'd swim more rivers. I'd watch more sunsets. I'd go more places I have never seen. I'd eat more real ice cream and fewer imaginary ones.

You see, I was one of those people who lived sensibly and sanely hour after hour and day after day.

Oh, I have had my moments, and if I had it to do all over again, I'd have more of those moments.

In fact, I'd try to have nothing but beautiful moments; moment, by moment, by moment.

In case you didn't know it, that is the stuff that life is made of – only moments.

Do not miss the now.

I have been one of those people who never went anywhere without a thermometer, a hot-water bottle, a bottle of gargle, a raincoat and a parachute. If I had it to do all over again, I would travel lighter.

If I had it to do all over again, I'd start barefoot earlier in the spring and stay that way later in the fall. I'd ride more merry-go-rounds, I'd watch more sunrises, and I'd play with more children.

If I had it to do over again – but you see, I don't."

> **I'D RIDE MORE MERRY-GO-ROUNDS, I'D WATCH MORE SUNRISES, AND I'D PLAY WITH MORE CHILDREN**

54 FACES OF AGING

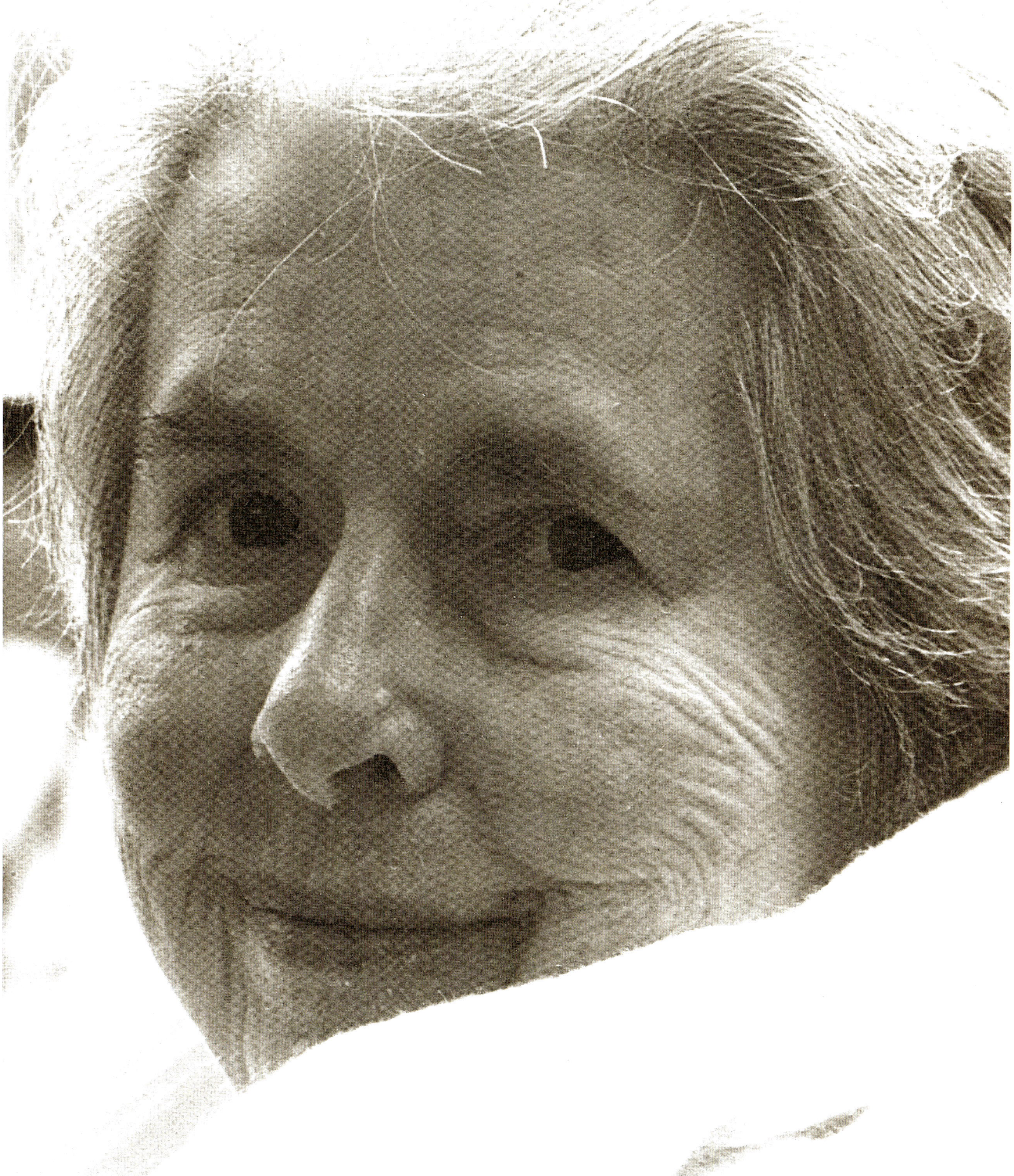

Beyond the Righteousness of Logic

In our younger years we would like to believe there is a certain logic to life and the way we live it. We plan our careers, families and vacations and feel that there is a way of doing things. But this attitude may change in our later years. Although we are just as likely to become more rigid in the way we approach life, we might also use our experience to prepare us to understand the complexity and multiplicity inherent in life and living. Life from the perspective of the older person allows for a more balanced assessment, allows us to see the meandering that occurs, the idiosyncrasies that defy any logic.

Know Thyself

The path toward understanding the human being — ourselves — is inexhaustible. It is a difficult journey to continue to explore yourself, to continue to question why you do what you do, why you think and talk and act in some ways rather than in others.

Through the commitment to continue to gain awareness about yourself and the world in which you live, you not only improve yourself and the world around you, you also set an example for generations to come. You make a commitment to stay alert, to keep your eyes peeled for the continual changes within and without.

Learning to Listen and Communicate

We can learn some practical skills to help facilitate understanding, learning and awareness. Most important, we can learn how to listen and how to communicate. This is especially crucial in our contact with the younger generations, who often want to voice their concerns and want to be listened to rather than to receive advice or admonishments.

Many of the problems that plague our planet — from international hostilities to political terrorism — could be lessened if only there were someone who would listen. And listening is not easy. It calls for compassion, detachment and trust. An elder who is able to listen can help different points of view unfold — however vague or one-sided they might be — believing that every one of them is important to the whole community. By listening and facilitating communication, an elder helps the community to learn more about itself, grow and develop.

Going More Slowly

Going more slowly means paying attention to all the many parts that make us who we are: the lover, the doer, the joker, the adventurer, the mother or father, the naïve, the wise, the academic, the child, the melancholic, and many, many other possible states and personalities. This means being as aware as possible of the richness of who we are and giving these parts equal priority as we move through our day and life.

How do things feel? For example, are we only paying attention to the doer and achiever and not making space for the player, the child, or the adventurer? Are we playing it too safe, or are we taking too high a risk?

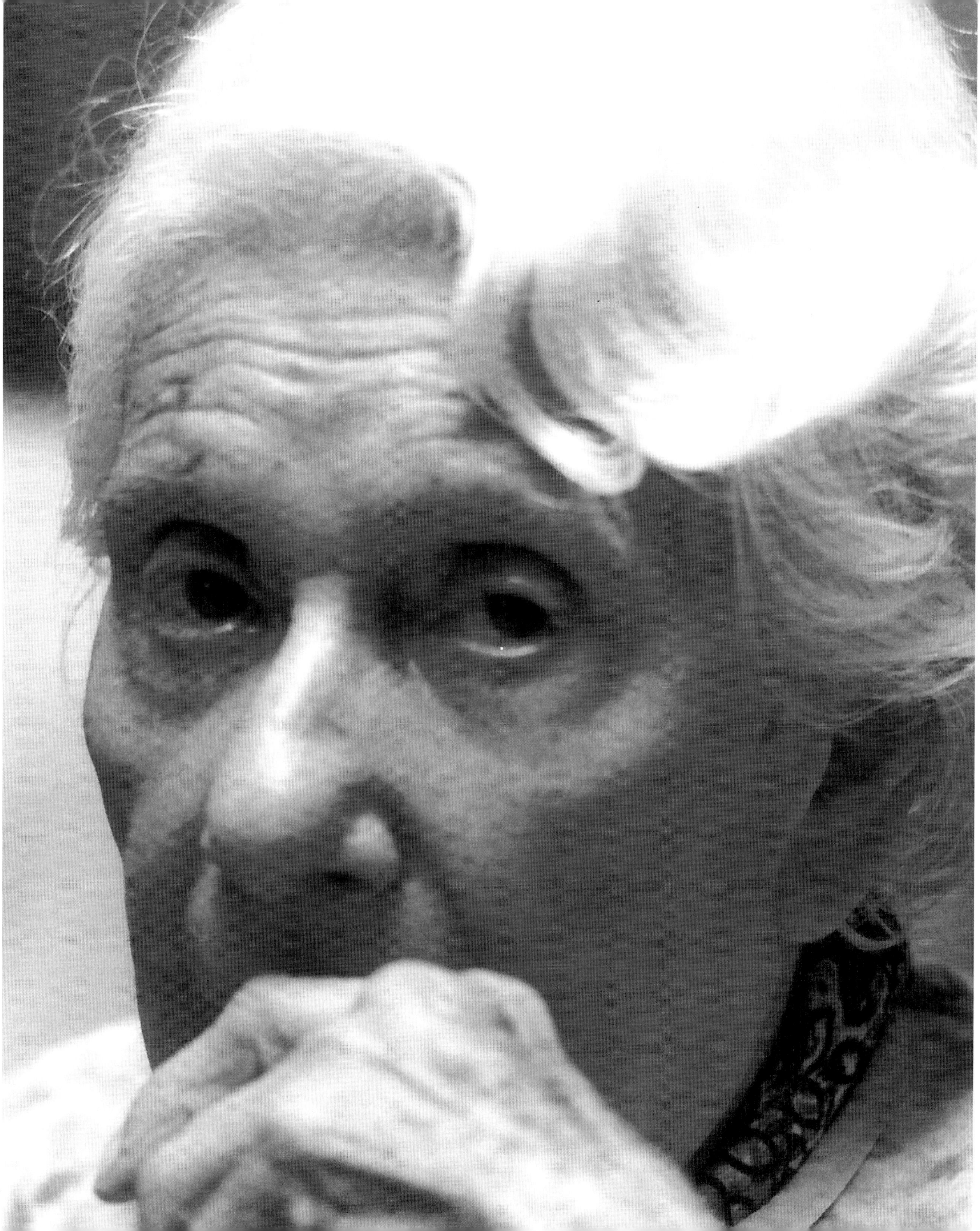

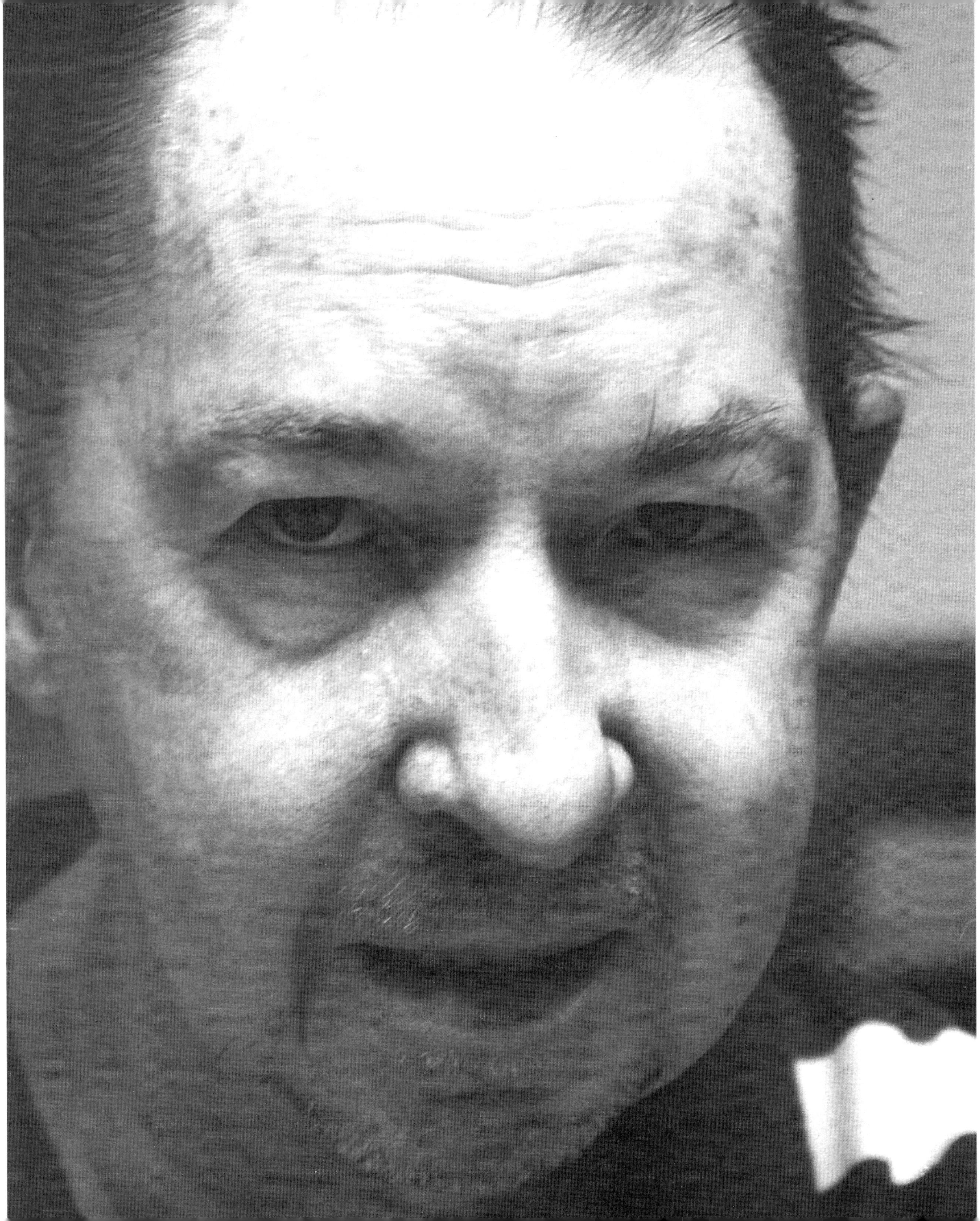

We need to step back from the material machinery of work and consumption; we need to ensure ourselves the time to slow down and listen to our heads and hearts – together.

As one American Indian allegedly exclaimed: "The white man is crazy; he thinks with his head and not his heart."

Be Alert: When Old Age is an Enemy

Just like any phase of life, old age has its dangers. Forget for the moment the dangers linked to society's demands to look young, fit, productive and fast. Think instead of the dangers that are deeply rooted in the archetypal or eternally valid aspects of the aging process. The negative aspect of the *Old Person* is represented by Saturn-Kronos, the mythical old god who would eat his own children. Thus he would not allow anything new to happen, would not allow the expression of a creative impulse, or the implementation of a new idea. The negative Old is rigid, righteous and closed-minded. This happens when just one side of the psyche rules unconsciously and despotically; a person is just old, and has lost touch with what is child-like within, with immaturity, with the eternally young spirit.

Old age can trap us in the form of a certain mood, a feeling that it is too late to do this or that, to start a new career, to learn another language, to organize a party, to get involved in a new relationship.[39] We might start to think that something would take too much effort or be too tiring. Why on earth would we want to take that trip to Italy, anyway? We don't have the energy we used to have, we feel low and can't access any inner creativity.

South American Indian tradition holds that there are four great enemies on the path to personal growth. We encounter *Fear, Power, Clarity of Mind* and, as already mentioned above, *Old Age*.

Most of us understand how *Fear* can be a potential enemy to personal growth. Fear can keep us from trying to live our life more fully, can be an impediment to understanding ourselves more completely.

Why *Power* should be an enemy is less obvious. However, power blinds us when we feel so powerful that we forget we are also weak. We have forgotten that there is great learning through accepting our weakness.

The same holds true for *Clarity of Mind*. If we believe that we are lucid and clear we can forget that we are also unclear. But life always holds surprises which we can only appreciate if we are open to them. *Clarity of Mind* can trap us in the belief that all is understandable, reasonable and evident. In contrast to this attitude, however, the wisdom of the ages and sages tell us that we live in a world full of mystery.

POWER BLINDS US WHEN WE FEEL SO POWERFUL THAT WE FORGET WE ARE ALSO WEAK

JEANETTE

*Jeanette's graceful face
beams gently when she speaks
of love. Her heart is nearly always full
to brimming like pond after rain
fed by incessant burbling springs.*

*And Life streams in from thawing snows...
she recalls her young husband, vigilant
in the hallways of their high school – protecting
the sweetness of his soon-to-be bride.*

*Or his return from war and the conception of their child.
Her eyes get quiet when she replays the words...
"you need a coroner, not a doctor" as the trauma
of his unexpected death is
healed a little more
in earnest whispers.*

*She wonders as she waits
if one day they'll know again
peace and safety
in the remembered embrace
of two who sincerely love...*

*A life romantic and brave
as the heroine in a paperback
book poised gently on her delicate lap
unfolds easily when she wants to talk.
Her children and grandson fill her eyes
with certain light, with pride
and with concern when one of them
is hurt.*

*She has loved so well and worries still
her mother's heart spreads wings that rise
as egrets in flight.*

*A woman's voice chides when she is teased by a friend
and the sometimes timid timbres sharpen with
the tones of northern New York... reminds me
of all she has left behind
and yet to know,
for sure.*

FACES OF AGING

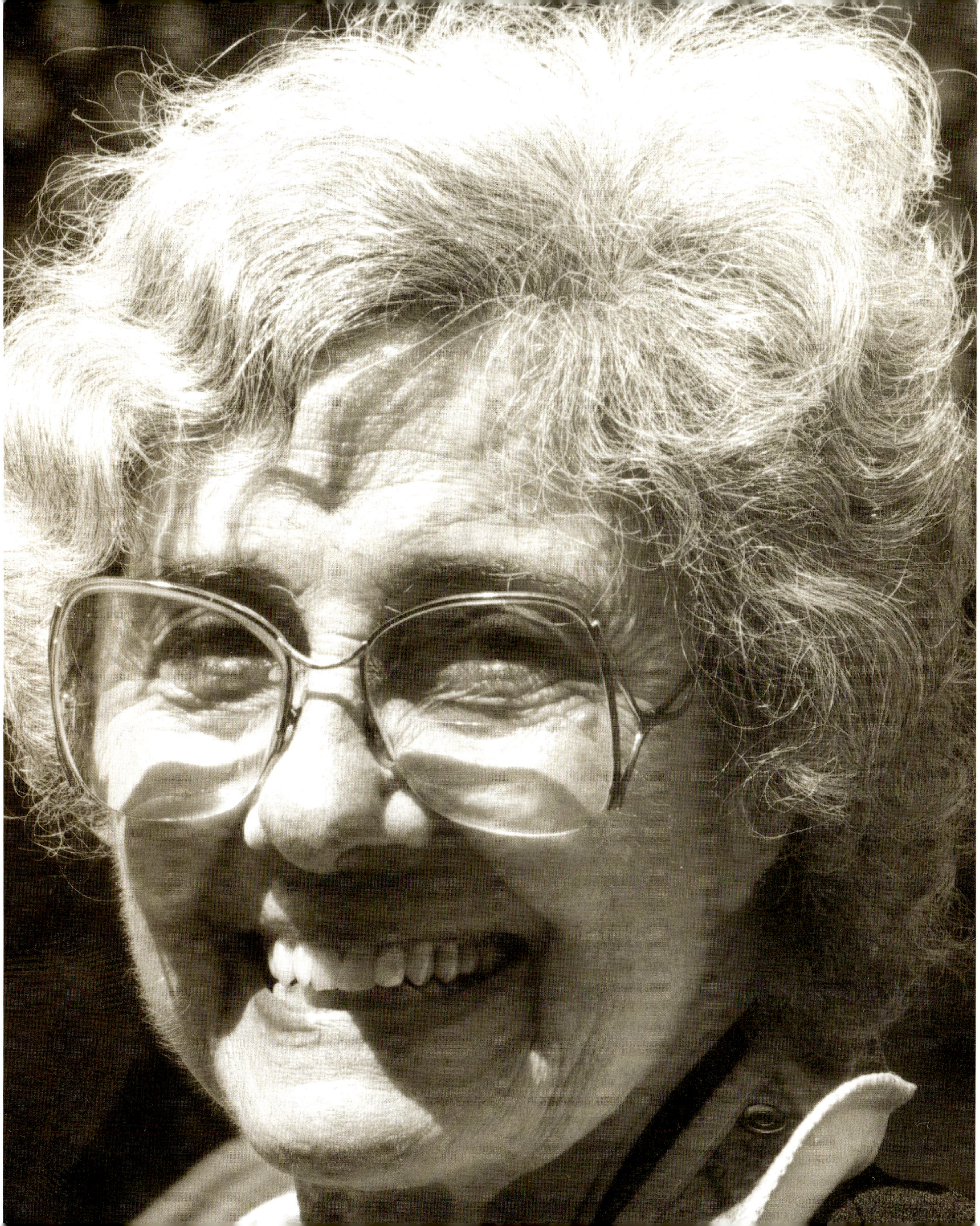

JUDD

Knows himself better
than any of us, too foolish to know
how crazy we are.
And can describe what often passes beneath the wire
of words.

So sensitive and attuned to his inner world,
he feels the ticking of currents
others might tune out
in the turning of busy circles.

How much a disappointment hurts, how envy stings like
a needle embedded in flesh - how hard to extract,
how a grudge makes a bear trap on the heart, and drives
a wedge between one
and the world.

As attuned as the yogi or
Zen priest to that which many seldom speak, his ashram
finds itself within these walls, where he meditates
upon this:
"How much excitement is it safe to feel?"
How low is too low?
" – This low?" he asks, raising an eyebrow and lowering his palm,
measuring the space between it and the ground...
"too low," he says and snatches it back up an inch,
"just right..." he smiles... "unless I need to sleep."
We share a knowing laugh at this.

Judd loves to read Heidegger - a line at a time.
Or, "a word at a time," he jokes, "when necessary."
He listens to jazz for solace and joy.
But his calm bearded face truly grins
when contemplating soft odd clouds in the distant sky.

On a long drive over the pass, our imaginations meet;
we find flying ships and fleets of saucers in the pastel strokes so far away
Winding through pines, heavy with snow, and we have time,

finally to talk together and to be.
Always, delight is punctuated by thought.

His smile contemplates a safe harbor now,
the simple affection of a friend.
In this abiding calm, he finds real peace
and holds the gift
with an open hand.

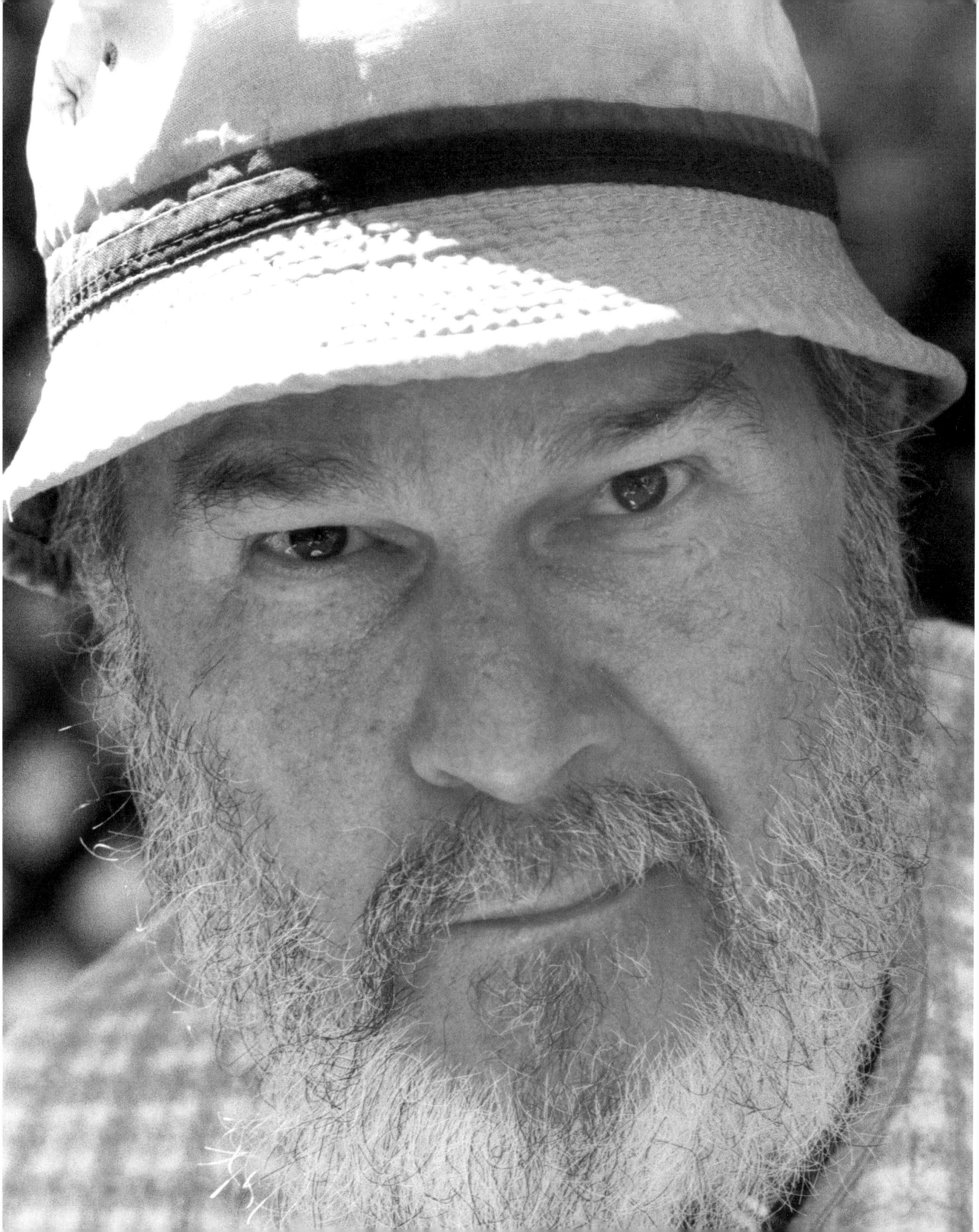

ELDERS ACADEMY

Imagine…

Imagine a place where the energy and the insight of the young and the wisdom and experience of the old both have a place in dialogue with the social mainstream. A place where our efforts to gain more awareness and become more in touch with our own inner components – and more detached from possessive emotions – are fully supported.

A place where we have a chance to discover what we have learned through life's good and bad and to use that knowledge to the benefit of our community, society and even the whole world. Where the elderly do not wield life experience as a weapon of intolerance in an argument, and the young do not use strength and energy as tools of oppression. Where we do not stop listening to other points of view and never stop trying to express our own views in a way that will help others transform as well.

Where the young start to believe in guidance again, because we are starting to learn how to guide without blocking. Where the old start to believe in their wisdom again, as they are challenged to share it and use it creatively to solve current problems. Where the young are supported in their journeys toward personal power and the elders are supported if they choose to relinquish their power and move towards other realms of interest and inquiry.

A place where learning – no matter how challenging it might be – is always fun. Where the spirit of our times, the *Zeitgeist*, and our passion guide the school curriculum.

A Vision For The Next Step

We live in a phase of history in which many of us devote little time to sitting back and thinking. We ought to reintroduce thinking to our lives; not the kind of calculative thinking common in normative science, but the kind of thinking that is creative and full of surprises. It is a thinking that stays connected not just to our inner elder, but also to the diverse beings that we all are.

How can we make this happen? How do we translate the ideas of eldership and conscious aging into everyday life?

These questions are the foundation of a new educational endeavor that we might consider here. Imagine calling this different place of learning *Elders Academy*.

Traditional schools and universities are meant to prepare us to play certain roles. We learn to become doctors, teachers, accountants, pilots, and so on. In Elders Academy, we want to learn how to become more aware of the various roles that we play and how to step back from them.

As much as we value traditional knowledge, we also want to learn to forget what we know and retain the fresh outlook of the "beginner's mind." We want to learn and teach how to be open to various processes that are unfolding.

For example, students with a strong urge or desire to somehow make a difference in the world – perhaps they want to help poor

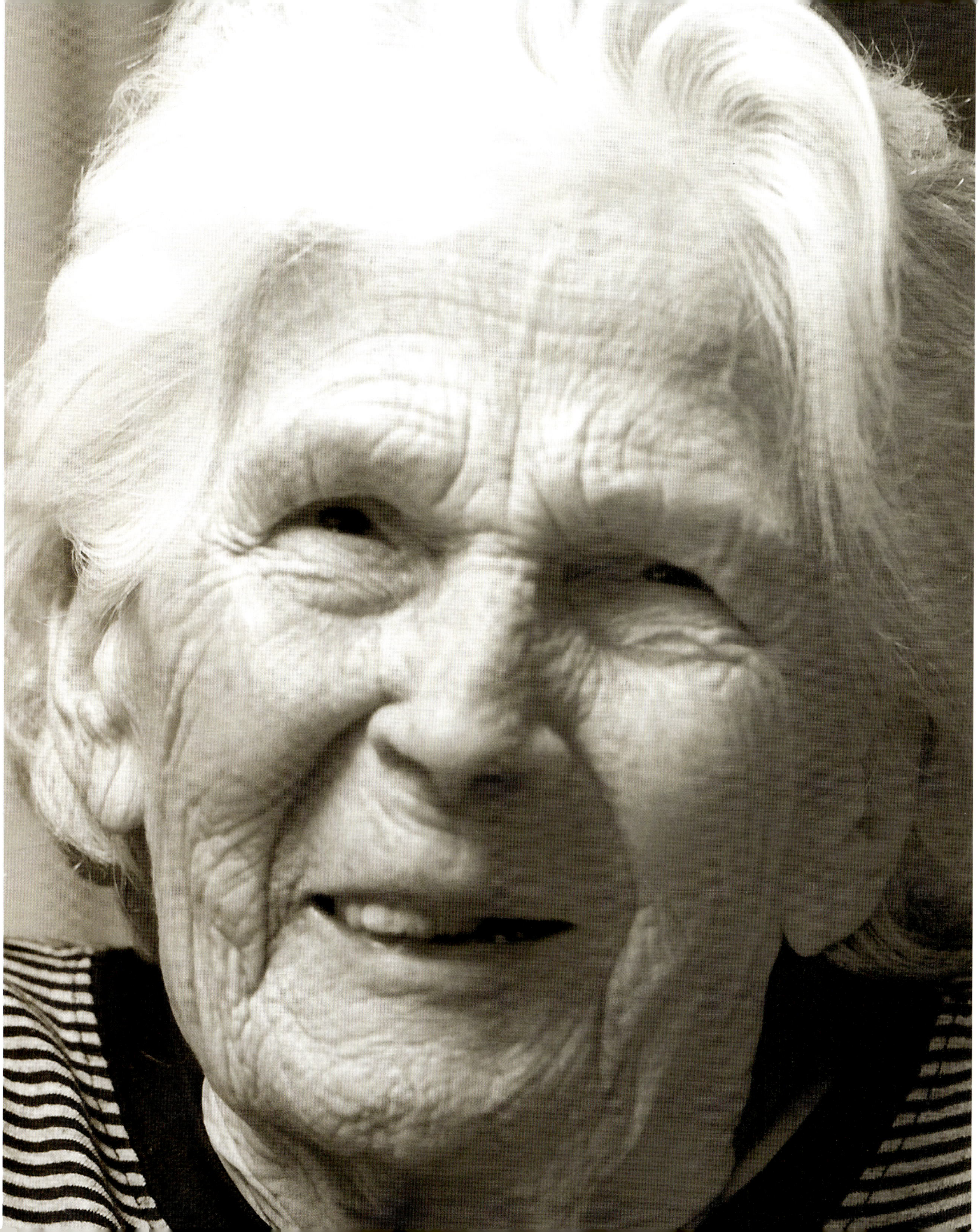

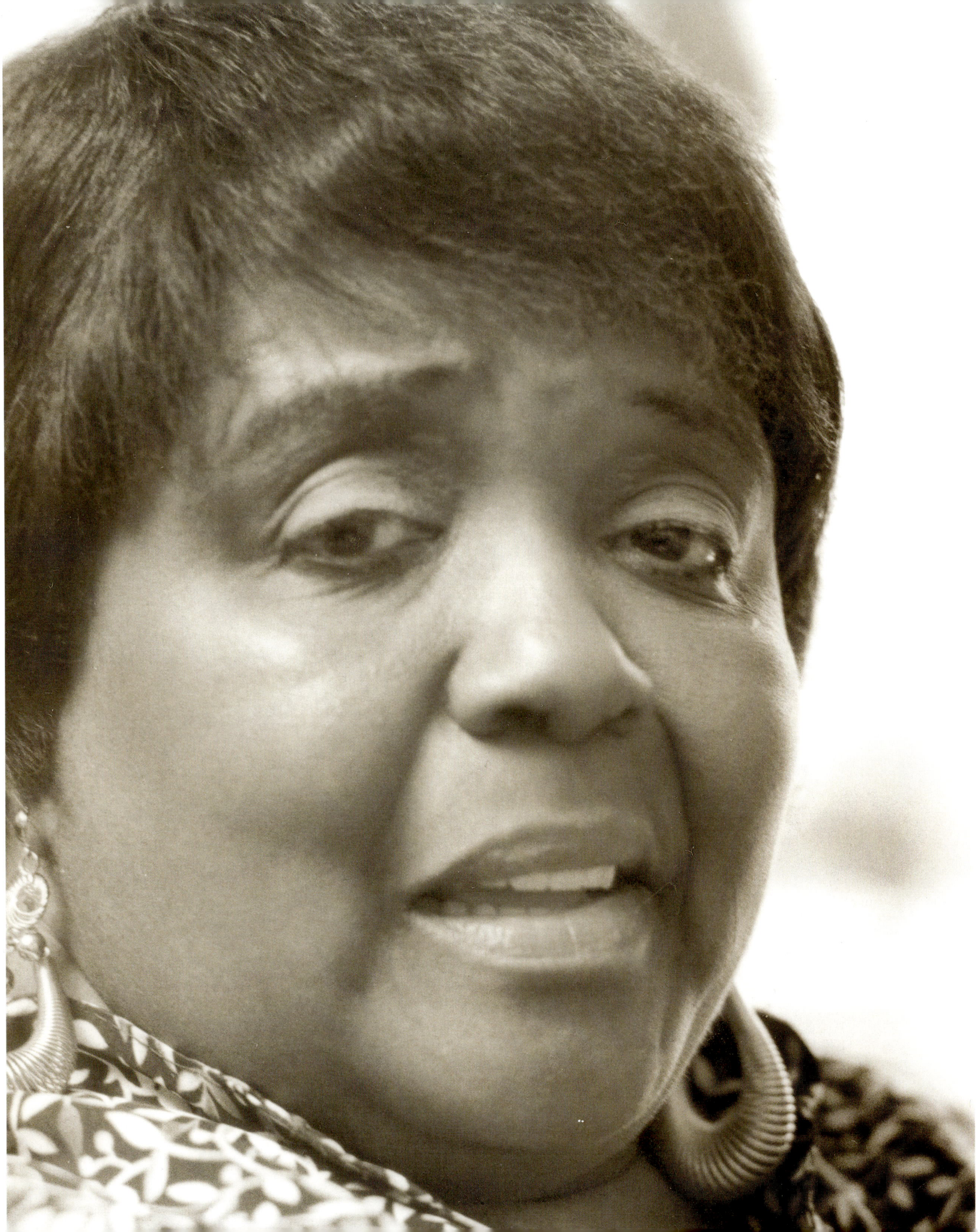

people somewhere, want to fight against injustices they perceive, help in protecting the environment — are met in their ambitions. Their passion is not diminished by preconceptions of what students ought to learn and know, of what is possible and not possible, of what is acceptable and not acceptable. Their feelings, experiences and ideas are validated as important and form the foundation of their continued and deepening education — true to the etymological origin of the word "education." For "education" does not mean that a student is filled with information; in contrast, it means that an educator "draws out" what is already present within students and leads them towards an understanding of this innate knowledge.

This is a big shift. It implies that teachers do not profess to know. Rather, they see themselves, along with their students, on a long road of discovery and learning. Teachers model as much learning as they do teaching.

As some American Indians say, when you stop learning, life is no longer fun. Which is not to say that learning is a linear process of acquiring knowledge. We learn through our own experience, by reflecting upon what we do and who we are, by applying our ideas and beliefs, struggling with mundane events, coping with relationship challenges, being creative, being lost, or having fun. At Elders Academy, we would make space for various ways of learning, believing that content and method are interdependent. This means that *what we do* cannot be separated from *how we do* it. An example from education might be that if we want to teach students to be independent and critical thinkers, the way we teach this ought to mirror the content of what we want to teach. Or if we want to live a more peaceful life, the way we go about this is as important as our ideas about what we think the components of such a peaceful life are.

Imagine you had no opinions; you could see value in each of the many ideas about life you encounter. Imagine you remained tirelessly open and curious to learning about the challenges this world offers because you deeply felt life's mysterious quality. Imagine you felt content and at peace with yourself, able to accept who you are and who you are not, what you can do and cannot do — and held this attitude towards others as well. Imagine…

Elders Academy would be a place where we can learn — or, rather, find in ourselves — the qualities, attitudes and skills that elders possess. It would be a place to practice how to use these abilities during encounters with other generations and our selves, as well as the larger world community — a community very much in need of the awareness elders can offer.

NOTES

1. Paul Ray & Sherry Anderson, *Cultural Creatives*, Harmony Books, 2000.
2. Elizabeth Bugental, *Agesong* (unpublished manuscript); parts of this manuscript first appeared in *The Existential-Humanist*, Vol.2.2, 1997.
3. Knoblauch, *Elders on Love*, Parabola Books, 1999; 9-10.
4. Rabbi Zalman Schachter-Shalomi is co-author of *From Age-ing to Sage-ing*; quoted from *Elders on Love*, 1.
5. "Calling All Elders. An Invitation to the 'Second Adventure of Life.'" An interview with Michael Mead by Jane Lister Reis, www.newtimes.org.
6. Ram Dass, *Still Here*, Riverhead Books, 2000; 12.
7. Gunhild O. Hagestad, "Able Elderly in the Family Context," in: Elizabeth W. Markson and Lisa Ann Hollis-Sawyer (eds.) in: *Intersections of Aging*, Roxbury Publishing Company, 2000; 265.
8. Elizabeth W. Markson and Lisa Ann Hollis-Sawyer (eds.) *Intersections of Aging*.
9. "Japan's Honorable Elders," in: *Intersections of Aging*.
10. This is also referred to as the "birth cohort."
11. Mike Hepworth, "William and the Old Folks," in: *Intersections of Aging*; 30.
12. James Hillman, "Senex and Puer," in: *Puer Papers*, Irving Texas: Spring Publications, 1979.
13. James Hillman, *Kinds of Power*, Currency DoubleDay, 1995; 63.
14. ibid. 238.
15. In this discussion I am indebted to Benjamin Schlesinger's article, "The Sexless Years or Sex Rediscovered," in: *Intersections of Aging*.
16. "The Sexless Years or Sex Rediscovered," 53.
17. ibid.
18. ibid.
19. Schlesinger cites some facts about sexuality and aging: "People 65 and older are often having as much sex, and in some cases more than people aged 18-26." (The Janus Report on Sexual Behavior, 1993). Also: "Elderly people in Sweden who are sexually active have more vitality and better memories than celibate counterparts." (Toronto Star, Oct 11, 1986).
20. *Kinds of Power*, 207.
21. "The Age Boom," Jack Rosenthal, in: *Intersections of Aging*.
22. *Elders on Love*, 9-10.
23. A. Stevens, *Archetypes: A Natural History of the Self*, New York: William Morrow, 1982, p.159; quoted in *Elders on Love*, 18.
24. *Still Here*, 102.
25. Hillman states, "Because the pure in spirit do not submit to the common sense of prevailing consciousness, they seem to have cracked ideas and overly intense ways of behaving. Is this because they believe they really could change the world?" in: *Kinds of Power*, 202.
26. Mike Hepworth, "William and the Old Folks," in: *Intersections of Aging*; 31. Hepworth also notes the tendency among caregivers to infantilize the old. He states the reason for such infantilization as follows: "It is precisely because infancy and childhood have, since Victorian times, been socially constructed as stages of legitimately innocent and beguiling dependency that this metaphorical transformation is an effective technique for containing and dispersing the fear of old age which is endemic in western culture." 31.
27. The absurdity is especially evident in how many physicians must "care" for their patients in well-timed cycles, sometimes as low as a few minutes.
28. *Elders on Love*, 5.
29. Lao Tzu, *Tao Te Ching*, transl. by Ursula K. Le Guin, Shambala, 1997; 77; verse 59, "Staying on the Way."
30. Rebecca Latimer, *You're Not Old Until You're Ninety*, Blue Dolphin Publishing; Nevada City, 1997.
31. Michael Mead, "Calling All Elders."
32. Arnold Mindell, *Sitting in the Fire*, Lao Tse Press, 1995; 184. Robert's Rules of Order are a set of fixed rules to which organizational meetings must adhere.
33. Baba Yaga by *Anonymous*, www.mythinglinks.org
34. *Still Here*, 90.
35. ibid. 133.
36. *You're Not Old Until You're Ninety*
37. linked to humility by its etymological root of humus, meaning "earth."
38. *Still Here*, 79.
39. The concept of aging as a mood was presented by Arnold Mindell and Max Schupbach during seminars in 2001.
40. James Hillman, *The Force of Character*, Random House, 1999.

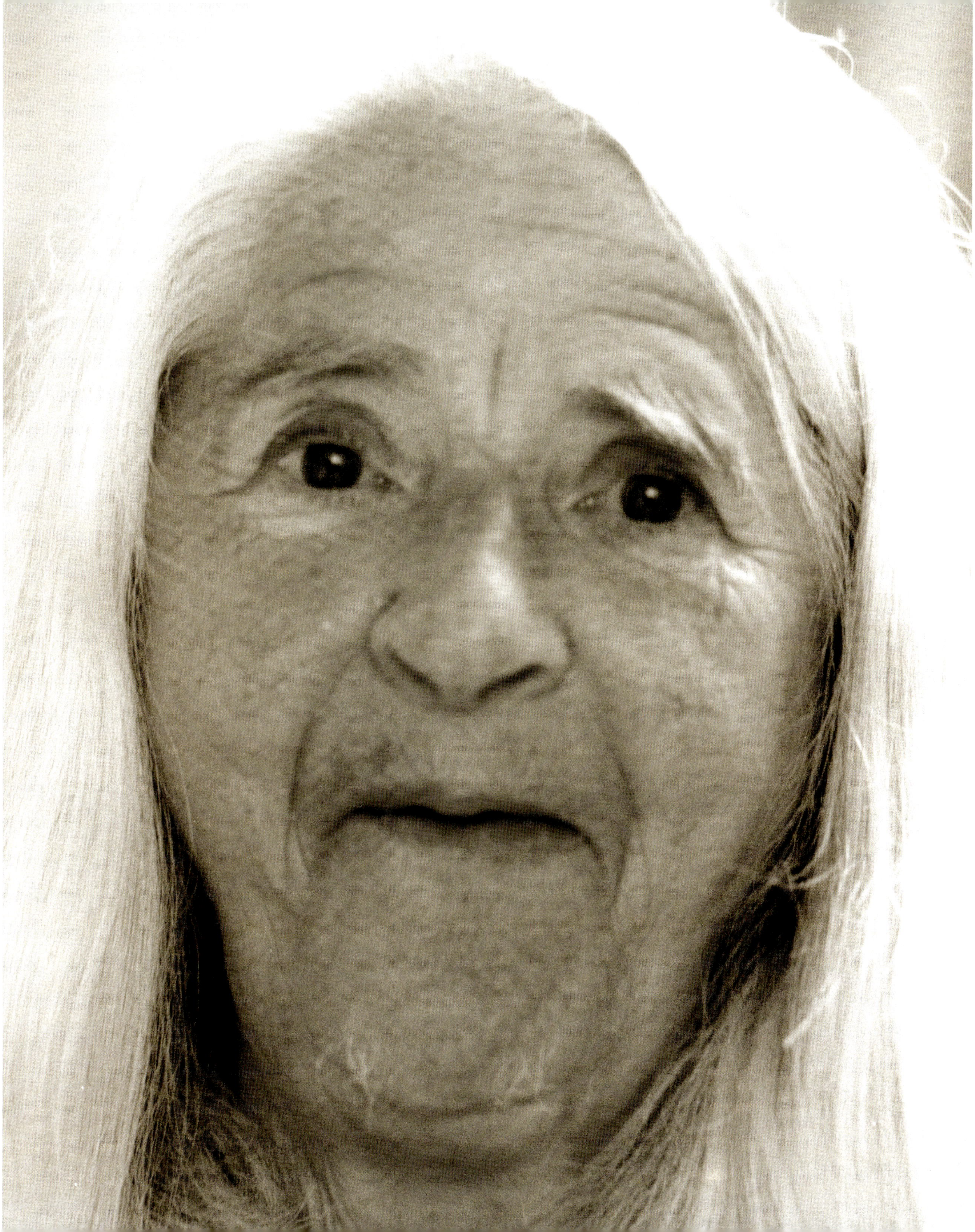

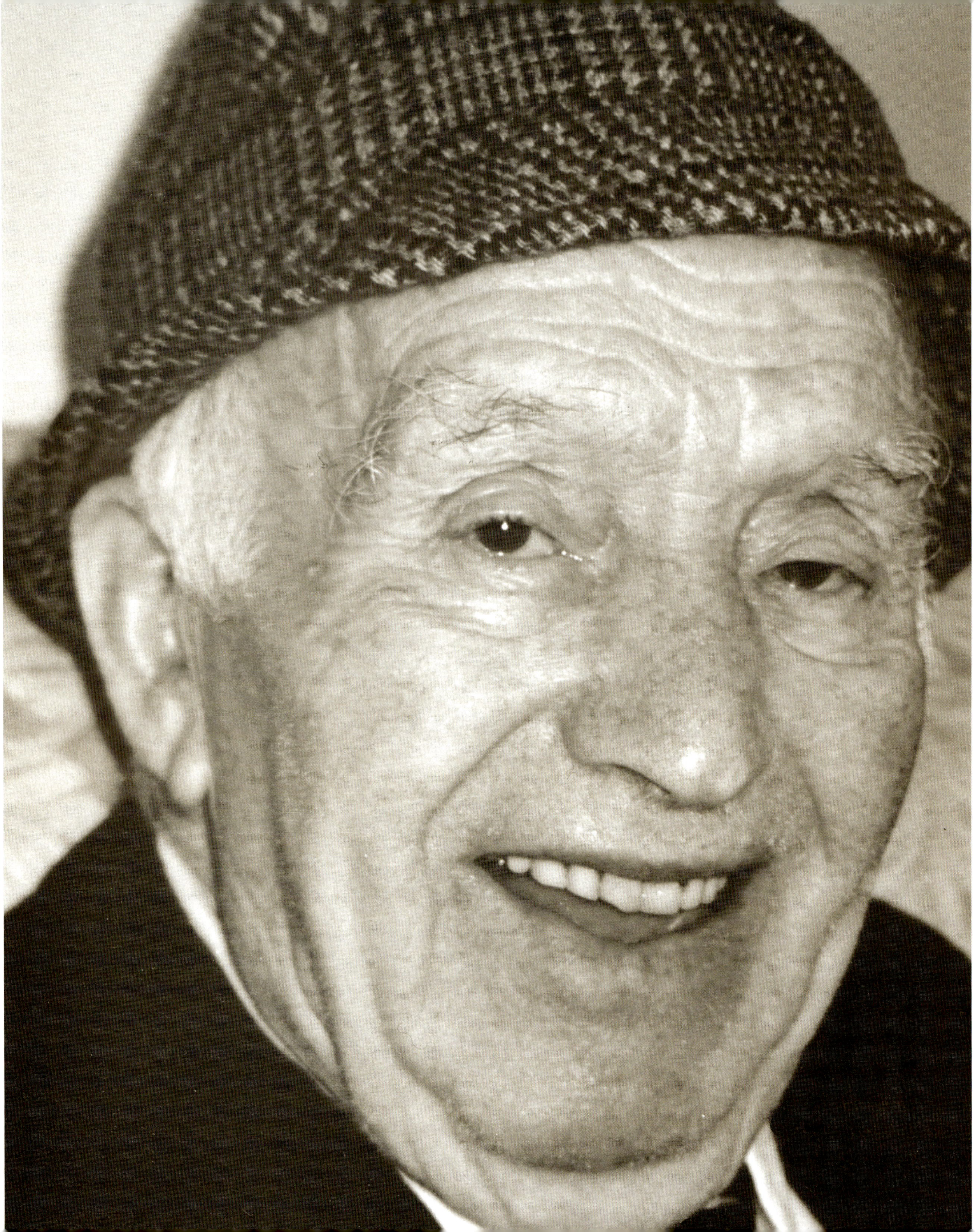

ACKNOWLEDGEMENTS

One evening, in the middle of building Hayes Valley Care, my brothers and I were sitting in our small 16th Street apartment in San Francisco feeling amazed that we had just received a phone call from another person wanting to help us. Offers like this just when we needed them most were too numerous to be pure coincidence. We began to see ourselves guided and assisted by some greater spirit – or *el spirito grande*, as Katuza, that loving and crazy Mexican shaman, taught me to call it. All we had to do, it seemed, was to have faith in the importance and value of our vision and pursue its implementation.

Along this path of faith in our *idea*, we were helped by many beautiful people who directly and indirectly made Hayes Valley Care and this book possible. To the degree that my memory allows, I would like to thank and mention them here.

Foremost among these I owe my deepest gratitude to all of the elderly for the learning and growing they have afforded me over the years.

This gratitude also extends to those who trusted Hayes Valley Care – the new kid on the block – to provide the kind of care it promised to provide: to the family members, conservators, social workers, discharge planners, doctors, guardians and therapists – thank you for your trust.

Because this book is grounded in the very existence of Hayes Valley Care, I am especially grateful to all the people without whose help Hayes Valley Care could not have been built: to Thomas Klausmann from Suppenkueche, who helped identify the building in the early stages; to Masha Levison whose tenacity and wit propelled the project forward; to Earle Mills and Ricardo Hernandez, who taught me much with their amazing dedication to caring for the elderly; to Papa Don Wilson, who was sufficiently crazy to support the dream financially and round-up a full soccer-team of others to support this vision; to the Gaehwiler construction team, especially Jimmy Joyce, who remained steady throughout many of the project's crises; to Jim Stavoy and Steven Whitney, who were always willing and able to translate ideas into seemingly endless architectural revisions; to the City of San Francisco, especially David Lally, who believed in the mission of Hayes Valley Care from the very beginning and cared for us in so many ways throughout the years; to Tom Mesa, whose creative spirit brought "health" to "health care" again; to the caring people of the Community Mental Health System; to Joanne Wyle and the dedicated team of Community Focus; to sister Elke and partner Chad Lewis, who joined our team to continue to extend the vision of respectful care for the elderly; to Cliff and Julia Landis, for their deeply felt poetry in this book as well as their enthusiasm for working with the elderly; to Patrizia Sandoval, whose huge heart was always ready to support and help no matter what time of day it was; to Will Clayton, who endured countless hours of revisions and editing throughout the years and helped put this book together; to Karla Kennedy and the Blue Mountain Center of Meditation, especially Nick Harvey and Christine Easwaran, who helped in giving us the confidence to begin our spiritual program and set us on the path to "practice" – hard to imagine our present lives without their loving care; to the merchants and people of Hayes Valley, this great community of people who welcomed us with open arms.

And there are many others who helped make Hayes Valley Care a safe and heart-full place to live – to all those not mentioned directly here, I offer my heartfelt thanks.

I want to express my gratitude here to those people who helped lay the foundation of the vision behind Pacific Institute and Hayes Valley Care, who were mentors and elders, spirits of various sorts.

Foremost, thanks to Richard Wiseman and Dale Mackley who have always believed in me, the person, even when they had no idea what I was up to – their big hearts and steady support have taught me, more than anything else, the meaning and importance of eldership in human life; to Helga Dougherty, another elder, with her selfless, caring ways of being and her inimitable good German cooking – thanks for all your love throughout the decades; to Jim Bugental for his deep commitment to teaching urgently needed ways of helping and for giving me a way to translate existential ideas into actual practice; to the team of the Existential-Humanistic Institute, for their great support throughout the challenging beginnings; to James Hillman, whose brilliance continues to stir my passion and boggle my mind – his many *ideas* gave grounding to this book and continue to add excitement to my life; to Stanley Keleman for his pioneer spirit, his ideas on maturity and the life of the body; to my students and clients for their teaching and the joy they have given me, for pushing me to clarify and articulate my thoughts.

Special thanks to the team of Pacific Institute, an organization that sister Elke once called the "soul of Hayes Valley Care." Pacific Institute was founded by a group of enthusiastic psychotherapists and visionaries who continue to believe in an existential-humanistic, process-oriented way of looking at life, continue to dare thinking the thought that each human life is foremost poetic in nature and beautifully complete as it is – thank you for making Pacific Institute possible throughout the years, to the members of the Board, the supervisors, the many interns – especially John Wiser, our first intern in the gerontological program, first at Sutro Heights then at Hayes Valley Care, who stuck with us throughout the tough beginnings – thank you for all the years and memories; and to Padma Catell for coming on board and helping us run an ever more professional psycho-spiritual program for the elderly.

I am grateful to my partner Bogna for helping me in countless ways with this book, for her beautiful mind, her loving patience and tireless teachings; and to Julia and Paulina, the brightest and nuttiest ten-year-old elders West of this solar system; to Steve Owad, Emi Bulman and Piotr Orlik for their great help in editing and finalizing this book; and to my mother and father, who each in their own unique ways gave birth to what was, is and wants to be.

Final thanks to my two bros, Ali and Amir: their faith, trust and love are simply a treasure beyond compare; and to *el spirito grande* who holds and guides everything – past, present and future.

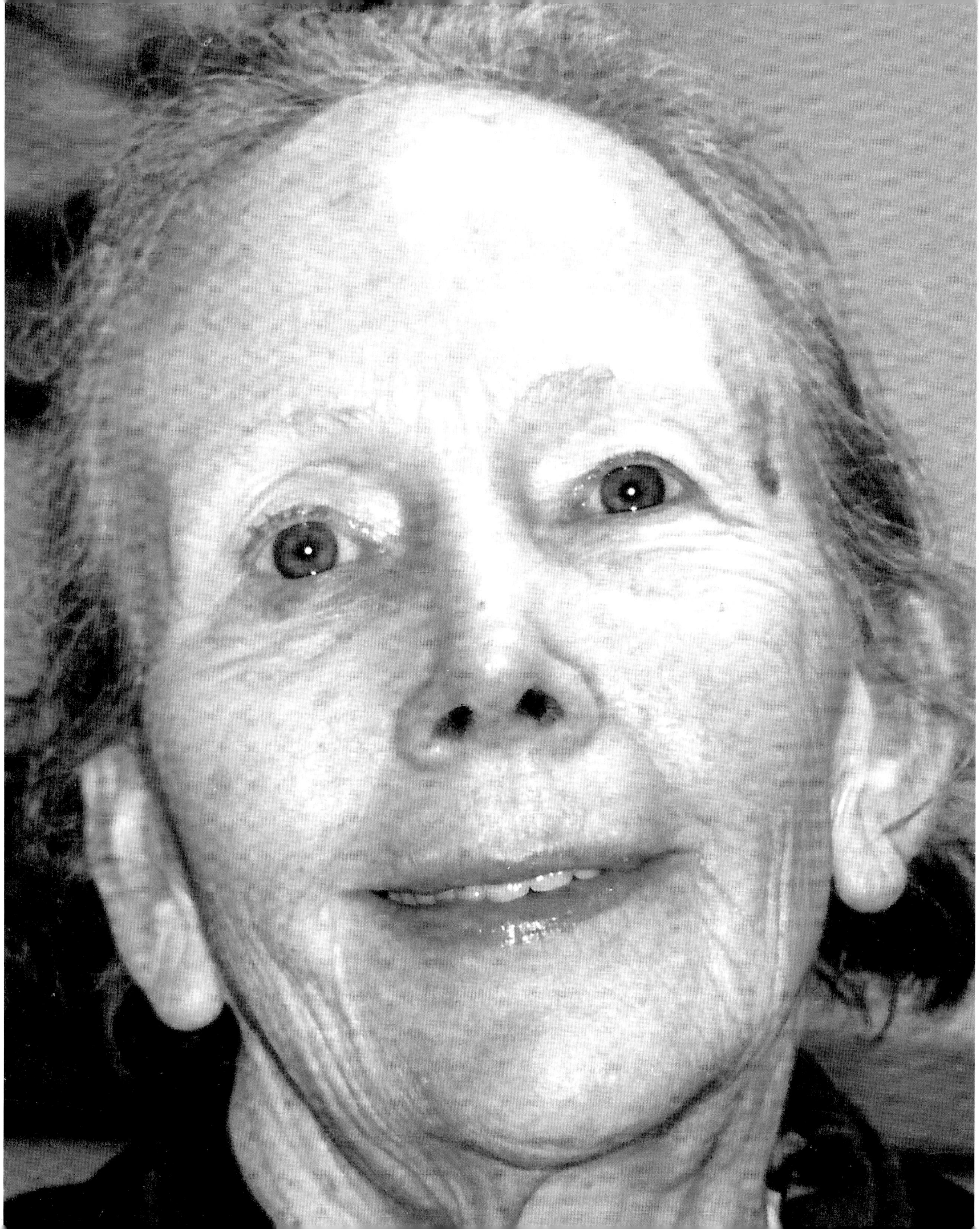

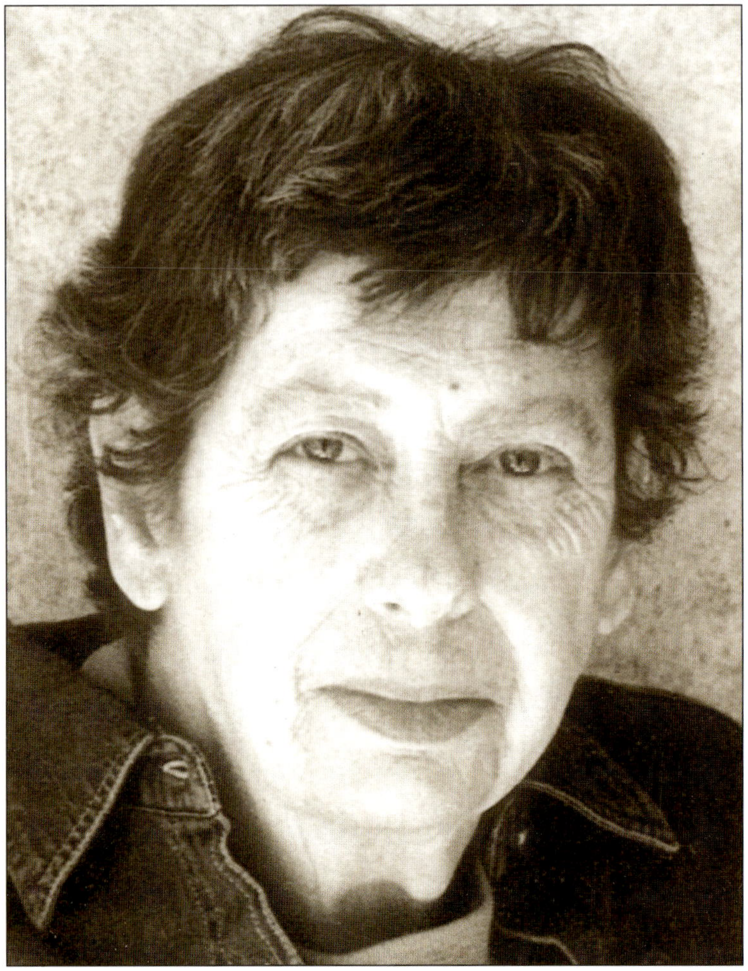

This world is a tree to which we cling –
we, the half-ripe fruit upon it.
The immature fruit clings tight to the branch
because, not yet ripe, it is unfit for the palace.
When fruits become ripe, sweet, and juicy,
then, biting their lips, they loosen their hold.
When the mouth has been sweetened by felicity,
the kingdom of the world loses its appeal.

~Rumi

Yes, old age is affliction –
especially, it is afflicted with the idea of affliction.
As long as we regard each tremor,
each little liver spot, each forgotten name
as only a sign of decay,
we are afflicting older age with our minds
as much as our minds are afflicted by older age.
The very repetition of our negative diagnosis
of what's happening to us each time
we see our face in the mirror
shows how powerful is the idea
to which we have harnessed our later life.

~James Hillman[40]

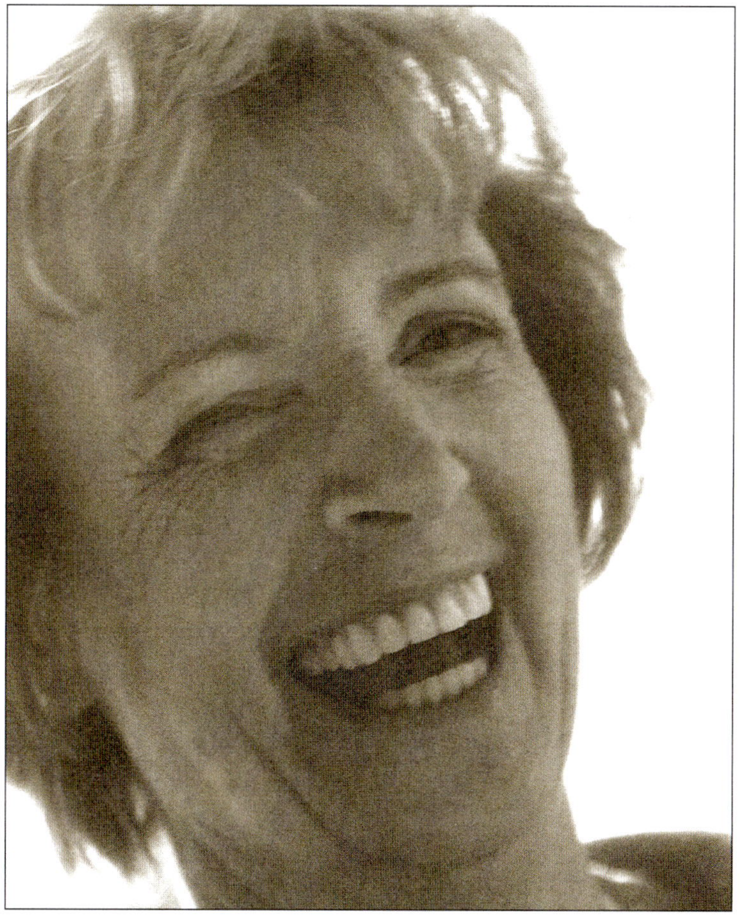

Elders Academy Press

Elders Academy Press would like to help in developing a vision of a contemporary Elder, a person (or role) we are longing for in our turbulent times – someone who is able to embrace our differences, hopes, dreams and failures.

We would like to search for a clearer understanding of what this Elder might be by promoting ideas and values such as:

> learning to listen to the voices from within and without ourselves;
> being open to not-knowing and to the mysterious quality of life;
> responding consciously to the world as it is, not as it should be;
> making room for wisdom in our lives by going deeper into events;
> trying to understand the language of symptoms as guides for our lives;
> allowing space for questioning dominant models of life;
> changing patterns of automatic and reactive behaviors.

Because we live in a time where Time itself has become important to understand, we would like to make space for questioning our relationship to time, what Time does to us, what we do to Time.
This questioning encompasses also the desire for understanding our meaning and purpose, for looking at life from the different viewpoints and attitudes given by our many cultural, intellectual and spiritual traditions.

Elders Academy Press is a publishing house of **Pacific Institute** and **Pacific Institute Europe**, both non-profit, public service organizations.
For more information please visit **www.pacificinstitute-europe.org**

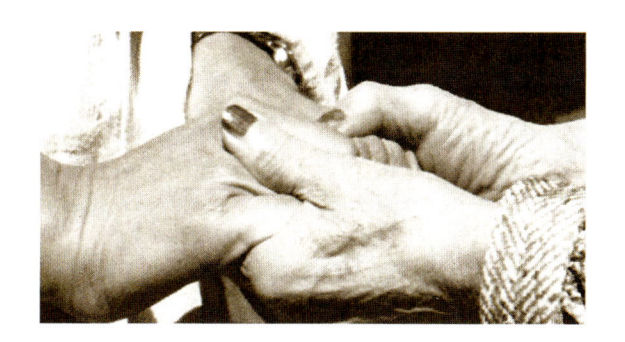

RENNER LEARNING RESOURCE CENTER
ELGIN COMMUNITY COLLEGE
ELGIN, ILLINOIS 60123